James Joyce

Titles in the series Critical Lives present the work of leading cultural figures of the modern period. Each book explores the life of the artist, writer, philosopher or architect in question and relates it to their major works.

In the same series

Michel Foucault
David Macey

Jean Genet
Stephen Barber

Pablo Picasso
Mary Ann Caws

Franz Kafka
Sander L. Gilman

Guy Debord
Andy Merrifield

Marcel Duchamp
Caroline Cros

Frank Lloyd Wright
Robert McCarter

Jean-Paul Sartre
Andrew Leak

Blackburn
College

Library
01254 292120

REAKTION BOOKS

To Rory

Published by Reaktion Books Ltd
33 Great Sutton Street
London EC1V 0DX, UK

www.reaktionbooks.co.uk

First published 2006

Printed and bound in Great Britain
by Cromwell Press, Trowbridge, Wiltshire

British Library Cataloguing in Publication Data
Gibson, Andrew, 1949–
    James Joyce. – (Critical lives)
    1. Joyce, James, 1882–1941 2. Joyce, James, 1882–1941 – Criticism and
    interpretation 3. Authors, Irish – 20th century – Biography
    4. Politics in literature 5. History in literature
    I.Title
    823.9'12

ISBN: 1 86189 277 2

Contents

Introduction by Declan Kiberd   7

Abbreviations   10

1   History, Politics, the Joycean Biography   11
2   Parnell, Fenianism and the Joyces   18
3   Youth in Nineties Dublin   27
4   An Intellectual Young Man, 1898–1903   35
5   The Artist as Critic   42
6   16 June 1904   50
7   Continental Exile   60
8   Looking Back: *Dubliners*   68
9   A Second Outpost of Empire   77
10   The Battle of the Book   89
11   Ireland Made Me: *A Portrait of the Artist*   95
12   Joyce, Ireland and the War   107
13   Writing *Ulysses*   115
14   The National Epic   121
15   Monsieur Joyce in Paris   132
16   Joyce and Free Statehood   138
17   Joyce Enterprises   145
18   A Wild, Blind, Aged Bard   151
19   The Megalith   157
     Endpiece   170

     Chronology   172
     References   179
     Select Bibliography   184
     Acknowledgements   190
     Photo Acknowledgements   191

James Joyce, *c.* 1917.

Introduction

Declan Kiberd

How did a city as sleepy and provincial as Dublin in the early twentieth century generate the extreme modernity of forms to be found in the writings of Yeats, Beckett or, most of all, Joyce? One answer might be that a colony is always a laboratory in which new methods are put to the test. Another might be to suggest that Irish artists had no superstitious investments in traditional English forms, which they felt quite free to pulverize. These analyses were explored with a sort of dignified audacity in Andrew Gibson's magisterial *Joyce's Revenge*, a book that helped to illustrate the ways in which *Ulysses* might have constituted a 'Fenian attack' on English cultural values. That such a study had been propounded by a leading English intellectual added a delicious layer of irony, much savoured in Ireland. Gibson's patient and richly detailed historical analysis – itself in the best traditions of British empiricism – helped to explain why the writers of his own country had found it so difficult to come to terms with Joyce.

In this intrepid new book, Andrew Gibson extends that investigation. Past biographers have assumed that Joyce became European and modern to the extent that he transcended his Irishness, but what if that story were to be told the other way around? Gibson assumes that to have been born Irish in 1882 was to have been modern anyway: rather than mapping elements of Joyce's life in continental Europe back onto the native island, he boldly takes the Ireland of Joyce's youth as a test-case for the modern world.

He works outward from that spot, as did Joyce himself. Gibson's artist is no languid aesthete or trifler with forms, but a man with a mission – to explore the ways in which he might liberate himself from all constricting codes, political, religious or artistic. The brilliantly innovative reading of *Exiles*, Joyce's only play, is but one vivid illustration of that search.

'Joyce went global', avers Gibson, 'before the world did'. If imperialism was itself a worldwide affair, then so also was the system of resistance. Parnell and de Valera became models for a Nehru or a Gandhi, as surely the politics of economic boycott became (in Joyce's own words) 'the highest form of warfare'. Gibson rightly contends that the global Joyce of postcolonial theorists is therefore an expression of the Irish experience rather than a release from it: but his project is also to challenge the merely internationalist Joyce still beloved of Parisian intellectuals, metroMarxists and North American professors with a more Hibernian type of thinker. He explains very well how Joyce himself connived for short-term tactical reasons in the international sensation of *Ulysses*, providing early commentators with the Homeric analogies so that the readers baffled by the sheer density of Dublin detail might find comfort in the thought that the core of the book was its European theme.

Throughout this luminous study, Gibson insists on Joyce as an example of the artist as thinker. His Joyce was a critic long before he became a poet or novelist. Taking a surprising but apposite cue from Joyce's comments on George Meredith, Gibson shows how *Ulysses* is one of those novels that might also be read as a philosophical essay.

The strength of Gibson's scholarship lies in his confident grasp of the social, intellectual and religious details of Anglo-Irish history, science and material culture out of which Joyce's work sprung. Much of his research was done in the decades when Irish scholars brave enough to proclaim Joyce an anti-colonial author were likely to be accused of assimilating his work to the campaigns of the IRA.

Gibson, who remarks astutely on how good the English have been at concealing from themselves the effects of their own colonial violence, is only too well aware of how many Irish intellectuals have become ashamed of their own patriots as once they were of their greatest writers. The irony of this project is that is has taken an Englishman to restore to us a fully Irish Joyce-as-modernist. No wonder that, late in this book, Gibson (in a sly parody of Joyce's visiting English scholar, Haines) talks of reading as a 'kind of atonement' for the hurts of history.

If the 'internationalist Joyceans' have often been guilty of showing as little interest in Joyce's indigenous culture as was once displayed by British imperialists, is Gibson open to the allegation that his 'saving' of an Irish Joyce may simply compound the old problem of an English domination of all malcontent on Gibson's own chosen terrain? I hope not. His books on Joyce prove the mischievous contention of George Bernard Shaw that Ireland is one of the last spots on earth still generating the ideal Englishman of history.

Therein may lie the real reason for the long-standing interest of English liberals and leftists in Ireland. For England, too, has an unresolved national question, postponed and deflected for almost two centuries by the idea of 'Britain'. A study which shows how a radical Dubliner worked for the spiritual liberation of his people might have much to teach those English who want to return to the project of William Blake and Percy Bysshe Shelley.

Though he knows that the British presence in Ireland was based on wrong-doing and sustained by violence, Gibson is never more forceful than when he shows us how caustic was Joyce's treatment of narrow-gauge nationalists in Dublin, who mimicked the worst excesses of Little Englanders. It may well be that his own rereading of Joyce's masterpieces is a chapter in the moral history of England and of its liberation too.

Abbreviations

WORKS

cw	*Occasional, Critical and Political Writing*
d	*Dubliners*
e	*Exiles*
fw	*Finnegans Wake* (followed by page and line number)
l	*Letters of James Joyce* (followed by volume and page number)
p	*A Portrait of the Artist as a Young Man*
sh	*Stephen Hero*
sl	*Selected Letters*
u	*Ulysses* (followed by page and line number of the Gabler edition)

OTHER

jj	Ellmann, *James Joyce* (revised edition)
pe	Potts, ed., *Portraits of the Artist in Exile*

1

History, Politics, the Joycean Biography

The sixteenth of June 2004 marked the centenary of the day, now known as Bloomsday, on which James Joyce's *Ulysses* is set. *Ulysses*, of course, takes place in Dublin, and to be in Dublin on 16 June 2004 was to witness a city seeming wholly gripped by the spirit and the works of its greatest writer. The largest and most ostentatious of the grand international Joyce conferences was in progress. Scholars from China to Peru were visible everywhere in Dublin: at formal occasions, in seminar rooms, on the streets, in bars. But the headiness of the occasion was by no means confined to an academic jetset. In the celebrating throngs outside the best-known Joycean pubs, the scholars were not especially noticeable. You would have been as likely to run into a Women's Reading Group from Copenhagen, some cheerful aficionados from Seoul or members of the James Joyce Appreciation Society of Vancouver, plus any number of miscellaneous Irish Joyce-lovers.

For Joyce's fame is extraordinary. He is the most illustrious literary figure of the twentieth century. He spans continents and cultures, worlds. The international Joyce industry annually pumps out more scholarly and critical work on its subject than any comparable behemoth in academic literary studies, with the exception of the Shakespeareans. Joyce also attracts amateur enthusiasts in larger droves than any other English-speaking author save, again, Shakespeare, or perhaps Jane Austen. Joyce went global before the world did. Those who write about him tend to assume that there

Bloomsday Centenary celebrations in Dublin, 16 June 2004.

was an irresistible logic to the process. The possibility was always intrinsic to the work: *vide* the number of languages in play in *Finnegans Wake*. The idea that the internationalization of Joyce and Joyce studies might partly have happened by accident, or that the factors that determined it were historical and political, would seem heretical to many (as a slur on Joyce's genius). From the point of view of the industry, it might even look ill advised (as likely to lead to a crash in the stock).

Yet the truth is that Joyce's posthumous reputation has been very much determined by historical events. Certainly, he left Ireland for Continental Europe at the age of 22 and, thereafter, never lived in his country of origin again. He saw himself as an exile and increasingly prided himself on his cosmopolitanism. But in the early twentieth century, as in preceding centuries, to be an Irish exile and even a self-exiled Irishman in Europe was to be something much more specific than a European, let alone an internationalist. Joyce did not so much set out to become a modern European genius as he was turned into one. This was the case, above all, in Paris, to which he moved in 1920, at precisely the moment when it had become the crucible of modernism in art, Joyce was swiftly co-opted for service as a hero of the modernist vanguard. That he not only consented to this but revelled in it, that it suited his own purposes very aptly, does not materially alter the point.

Joyce's Parisian career increasingly cast him as a modernist writer who happened to come from Ireland, as Picasso was a modernist painter who happened to come from Spain. The possibility that Joyce was in fact a fundamentally Irish writer, that, in the first instance if by no means exclusively, his work was always and everywhere concerned with Irish history, politics and culture, that what was taken to be its modernism originally expressed a specifically Irish-centred agenda, was seldom if ever entertained. The imperial Britain under which he had grown up tended either to misunderstand or to distrust him and his art, and had little interest in properly claiming him or identifying his aims. But an independent Ireland that had greeted the challenge of a new-found freedom by plunging into what Joyce saw as Catholic and nationalist reaction had still less. Few disputed the modernist appropriation of Joyce, and it blazed a trail for a second one. For before very long, America was saving Europe from itself.

The headquarters of the James Joyce International Foundation are in Columbus, Ohio. The most important Joyce periodical appears from Tulsa. If Joyce is an 'international' phenomenon, the majority of leading Joyce scholars are and have always been American. But the American pre-eminence in Joyce studies itself has a history. The American liberation of Europe and the Marshall Plan for its subsequent regeneration also had a cultural thrust. This was most obviously embodied in the Fulbright Act of 1946, which enabled the entry of American academic industries into Europe as never before. One consequence of the Act was that, in the phrase of American Joyce scholar Ellsworth Mason, the 'dissertationeers descended on Ireland like a plague of locusts'.[1] Ireland was fertile ground for literary

scholars: it had produced the most exquisite and demanding literature in English of the century, but had no developed native, scholarly
tradition to defend that literature or assert prior rights. For the
American scholar-pioneer, there was no more virgin land.

Two such pioneers were to prove particularly influential: Richard
Ellmann and Hugh Kenner. Ellmann was the most acclaimed Joyce
scholar of them all. His biography of Joyce was and still is regarded
by many as the greatest literary biography of the twentieth century.
He was an extraordinarily assiduous and painstaking researcher.
He appeared to set exacting, new, modern standards of competence
for the writing of literary lives. Ellmann's account of Joyce had
enormous weight and influence. Yet there was always a hole in the
middle of his narrative, a reason for nagging unease. Why had Joyce
bothered? What exactly was the great project to which Joyce had
sacrificed so much life, time, comfort, even health, and to some
extent, other people, including those he most loved? Ellmann's
massive and imposing volume was oddly short on answers.
Though age and success made him genial, Ellmann's Joyce was
vastly ambitious, self-absorbed, intent on his art. But this art was
apparently its own *raison d'être*. In the end, it was hard not to think
that Joyce the artist was chiefly powered by nothing more significant
than a personal aesthetic commitment, or even just vanity.

Kenner's Joyce was very different. But, though the two scholars
were very far apart, Kenner was also the necessary supplement to
Ellmann. For Kenner gave Joyce a cause. That cause was modernity;
modernity, however, as created and understood by what became
known as 'international modernism'. Kenner's Joyce belonged
with Nietzsche, Einstein, Heisenberg, Stravinsky, Pound and
Le Corbusier. He was one of the great champions of the modern
experiment with thought, the modern transformation of forms.
Joyce's was an art of the age of mechanical reproduction. It was even
a hi-tech art: the man who could work more than 60 languages
into *Finnegans Wake* clearly had a mind like a computer. Not

surprisingly, given his will to modernity, Joyce found Ireland small, backward, parochial, narrow, mean. Critics working within the tradition inaugurated by Kenner usually saw Joyce as indifferent if not actually hostile to his country and its people. There was even a moral justification for this view, given the supposedly unique blindness, crudity and recidivist violence of Irish nationalism. At best, Dublin and Ireland were raw material for Joyce's extravagantly innovative vision.

Thus Joyce, who had deracinated himself in one sense, was now cut off from his roots in others, too, and therefore left singularly exposed to historical circumstance. His work, it seemed, was boundlessly interpretable. The Kenner orientation set the trend: Joyce was claimed, simultaneously or in rapid succession, by myth critics, structuralists, post-structuralists, Marxists, gays, Deleuzeans and postmodernists, to name but a few. He could be read in relation to any historical context, from Paris '68 to Ground Zero 2001. If HCE in *Finnegans Wake* stood for Here Comes Everybody, then everybody came trooping to the wake. Everybody could have their piece of the Joycean action. The logic to this seemed more or less cast-iron. Did Joyce's modern texts not also jump forwards in time? Weren't they postmodern in spirit, paradigms of a slipperiness often called indeterminacy or undecidability? Could meaning not be squeezed out of *Ulysses* or *Finnegans Wake* ad infinitum? Try sitting down with a reading group and arriving at a consensus about any line in either book. Joyce's work became the literary equivalent of a vast rainforest, a rich and seemingly unending resource. Joyce was playful, too, which seemed to license critical free play. That Joyce himself had said that he had a precise knowledge of what everything in his work meant – that a particular intention was buried in every word – did not serve as even a notional constraint.

The postwar American investment in Joyce was extremely good for his reputation. He would have welcomed it, and we owe it an immense debt of gratitude. Americans did – and continue to do –

the bulk of the important work. American libraries stored manuscripts and built archives. Scholars ransacked encyclopaedias, dictionaries, gave us the facts and tracked down allusions, pored over marginalia, piled note on note, explication on explication. They unpicked the cryptic or puzzling knots in Joyce's notoriously obscure writing. It was as though an enormous, dark, shy creature were being slowly dragged out of its labyrinthine burrow and into the light. Increasingly, too, the American industry became indistinguishable from a multinational one, with branches all over the globe. Some of the great Joyce institutions, like Fritz Senn's James Joyce Stiftung in Zurich, are not American at all. The marvellous new edition of Joyce's notebooks for *Finnegans Wake* is European in provenance. Joyce studies are an exploding galaxy. There is no likelihood that they will eventually disappear into a black hole of dogma or final certainty.

Yet, ironically, explosion led to implosion, too. The more we got to know about Joyce, the more it seemed that some aspects of his work might be a little more important than others, after all. The more the scholars filled in, the more substantial, in a sense, that Joyce's work became, the harder it seemed to deny that it might everywhere be addressing Irish themes and Irish questions. Furthermore, the postcolonial turn in literary theory and criticism started raising some very awkward issues. Might the Joyce industry be in danger of replicating the lordly superiority of the colonizer and his lack of feeling for the indigenous culture? It seemed possible, after all, that disengaging Joyce from Dublin was almost as perverse as uprooting Jane Austen from the home counties. Melville had taken the *Pequod* round the world, but that didn't stop *Moby-Dick* from being an authentically, richly American epic. Perhaps, after all, the international Joyce needed to be placed in relation to another Joyce who not only literally preceded him, but had what Joyce himself might have called a spiritual priority, the Joyce who got the Irish papers every day in Paris. 'Each day, and each hour of the day', said his Parisian friend Philippe Soupault, 'he thought of Ireland' (*PE*, p. 116). Perhaps the cosmopolitan logic of Joyce's work should be read in relation to an Irish logic. The global Joyce might even be an expression of the Irish one, not a release from him.

No biography of Joyce, however, has been written according to this assumption. There are some very good accounts of the Dublin Joyce, like Peter Costello's. But in a sense, no one has yet read Joyce's life other than backwards, from the truly significant, mature artist of Trieste, Zurich and Paris to the fledgling poised on the edge of the world, in little Dublin. Hence, while this book draws heavily and gratefully on previous biographies, it also tries to tell the story in a slightly different way.

2

Parnell, Fenianism and the Joyces

James Joyce was born into a middle-class Dublin Catholic family in 1882. There is a lot in Joyce's work that we can only fully understand if we are aware of the progress of his family during the 1880s and its relation to developments in Irish politics and changes in Irish culture during that decade. When Joyce was born, the family was prospering. Joyce's father, John Stanislaus, had recently become the landlord of property in Cork. He had just started a job, too, as a rate collector with the Dublin civil service. This was a sufficiently distinguished appointment to require the approval of the British Chief Secretary of Ireland. It also paid very well. The Joyces could feel that they had entered the wealthier spheres of Dublin society. They could afford servants. They had smart friends. In the late 1880s John had even moved the family out of Dublin to a big house in affluent, genteel Bray. The civil servant became a commuter. He was particularly fond of James, his eldest living son. He was also ambitious for him, and sent him off to board at one of the best Jesuit-run Irish Catholic schools, Clongowes Wood College, to benefit from a gentleman's education. By the end of the '80s, however, John Stanislaus was drinking heavily and accumulating debts. In 1891 he had to take his son out of Clongowes. By 1893 he has lost his post with the civil service, come very close to bankruptcy and moved the family from the comfortable life of the southern Dublin suburbs to the bleaker life of the relatively impoverished north side of the city. The story of the Joyces in the '80s is very much the story of the first chapter of Joyce's *A Portrait of the Artist as a Young Man*, which takes us from a world of waxed moustaches, Eton jackets and sumptuous Christmas dinners to the 'vision of squalor and insincerity' with which the second chapter begins (*P*, p. 69).

The fortunes of the Joyce family in the '80s closely matched those of one man whose importance for Joyce was incalculable: Charles Stewart Parnell. James Joyce was born just as the Parnellite cause was starting rapidly to gain momentum; his last weeks at Clongowes coincided with the death and funeral of Parnell. With Daniel O'Connell – of whom more in a moment – Parnell was one of the two great Irish political leaders of the nineteenth century, a haughty, imposing Anglo-Irish aristocrat who won not only the awed respect of his countrymen and women but the admiration of many English, notably Gladstone. He was dedicated to the cause of an independent Ireland, at least, within the limits of the idea of Home Rule. He had served as Home Rule MP for Meath from 1875 and, in 1880, became Chairman of the Irish Parliamentary Party. Throughout the '80s, he worked, fought, plotted and schemed to dissolve the union of Britain and Ireland that had been established with the Act of Union in 1801.

Parnell appealed to his compatriots for many different reasons. They saw him as fiercely hostile to English political, economic and cultural interests. They appreciated his provocative 'obstructionist' tactics in the British Parliament, the fact that he so ruffled English feathers. They saw him as a great breaker of English rules. But he was also a radical exception to English stereotypes of the Irish. Irish politicians were supposed to be inflammable, easily roused and, therefore, easily manipulated. Parnell, by contrast, was cunning, unflappable, implacable. Joyce's father particularly admired Parnell's self-control, his habit of Olympian aloofness. Parnell was famous, too, for what his fellow Irish politician Tim Healy called his 'superb silences'.[2] Irish agitators were supposed to talk too much. Parnell was reserved, almost taciturn. He was particularly

'Nothing more singular can be imagined than the appearance of this intellectual phenomenon in the midst of the stifling morals of Westminster' ('The Shade of Parnell', *CW*, p. 194): Parnell expelled from the House of Commons for obstruction, 1881.

concerned with the low image (and self-image) of the Irish people, the fact that they were so often patronized if not despised. The Irish must discover their own authentic powers. Certainly, for the Irish in the 1880s, Parnell became the very figure for Irish pride, Irish self-assertion, Irish equality with England and, beyond that, the Irish presence on the international stage. As such, he was a driving force running through the aesthetics of the young and, to a very large extent, the mature James Joyce.

But in the last month of the 1880s, things changed. Parnell was cited as co-respondent in a divorce case in the English courts brought by Captain William O'Shea against his wife Katharine (the notorious 'Kitty' O'Shea). Gladstone quickly asserted that the scandal was endangering the alliance between the Liberal government in England and the Irish Parliamentary Party that he and Parnell had crafted together. The Irish Catholic church came out against

Parnell. The Irish Parliamentary Party that Parnell had so successfully welded into a serious political machine promptly split between
Parnellites and anti-Parnellites. The rift snaked its way through
communities and coalitions, families and friendships. The Ireland
Parnell had worked so hard to unite promptly tore itself in two.
No better picture of the passions thus unleashed exists than the
Christmas dinner scene in *A Portrait*, which pits the fictional version of John Stanislaus Joyce and his old friend John Casey against
respectable, middle-class, Catholic family friend Dante Riordan.
The result is a ferociously destructive confrontation in which
both sides are none the less bound together by the same agony
of disappointment.

John Stanislaus's trajectory followed Parnell's. One stratum of
the Dublin middle class was lodged quite safely in place. Its lot had
been improving since O'Connell and the Catholic Emancipation
Act of 1829. But Parnellism had also empowered another stratum
of Dublin Catholic society, to which the Joyce family belonged.
This stratum found its opportunity with Parnell's rise, and fared
well. But its social and economic prospects were curtailed with
his fall, and suffered an abrupt decline. Unlike the fathers of other
Catholic boys at Clongowes, nothing secured John Stanislaus's
prosperity, and he himself lacked the instincts to protect it. Parnell
died in 1891. John Stanislaus was among the many mourners who
stood in the rain to watch him interred in Glasnevin Cemetery in
Dublin. His own best hopes – and those of many of his friends, a
number of whom were later to make their appearance in *Dubliners*,
A Portrait and *Ulysses* – went to their grave with Parnell.

Hence the importance of the identity of John Casey in *A Portrait*:
Casey is a physical force man, that is, a Fenian. John Stanislaus had
not hurried to join the Parnellite cause. For reasons of both family
history and temperament, he was in some ways more drawn to
another political camp, that of the Fenians. To understand this,
however, we need to go some way back in Irish history. For in the

'Love and laud him' (*u*, 7.883): a Dublin crowd welcoming Daniel O'Connell outside the former seat of the Irish Parliament, 1844.

early decades of the nineteenth century, the great figurehead of Catholic Ireland had been O'Connell. O'Connell's power and persuasiveness had been such that he had pressed the English into emancipating the Irish Catholics. Joyce knew this very well, and has Stephen Dedalus pay O'Connell a handsome tribute in the seventh chapter of *Ulysses*. The homage is unsurprising: one of Joyce's ancestors had married into the O'Connell family in the 1840s. O'Connell stories were writ large in Joyce's father's early life, and father passed them on to son.[3]

But what loomed between O'Connell and Joyce and his father was the great Irish Potato Famine in the late 1840s. This had far-reaching consequences, many of which are important for Joyce's work. One was a radical anti-Englishness born of the sloth and gross incompetence with which the British government had responded to the catastrophe. This quite understandable if to some extent unhelpful hostility led directly to Fenianism. Fenianism was inaugurated in 1858, with the formation of the conspiratorial, oath-bound, secret society of the Irish Republican Brotherhood (IRB), or Society of the Fenian Brotherhood. The Fenians were (often romantic) nationalists who wanted an independent Irish republic, and were willing to think that it could be achieved by force. Many of the most important names in mid- to late-nineteenth-century Irish politics were associated with the movement, not least ones that figure in Joyce's writings, like James Stephens and John O'Leary.

John Stanislaus's grandfather was said to have been a member of the Whiteboys, an eighteenth and early nineteenth-century agrarian secret society that anticipated the Fenians. He was fiercely anti-clerical, and passed his anti-clericalism on to his descendants. Fenianism was gripping John Stanislaus's part of Ireland at the time when he was growing up. As a boy at St Colman's College, he came under Fenian influences. He had good friends who were Fenians, including gun-runners and dynamitards. In the 1870s he probably drilled and trained with Fenians.[4] His fictional self still uses mock-Fenian passwords in *Ulysses*. True, his new-found respectability in the '80s, along with his Parnellism, had put a distance between him and the rebel culture to which he had formerly been so close. But as *A Portrait* demonstrates, the old allegiances by no means faded away. In any case, in 1890, after the divorce scandal, Parnell himself pitched for the support of the Fenians in his struggle for political survival. He increasingly presented himself as having an intuitive grasp of the Fenian sensibility. He also took up the cause of the political prisoners, convicted Fenians and dynamitards, like the fictional John Casey, who were languishing in English gaols. He came close to thinking of Fenianism as the very heart of Irish nationalism. Fenians responded in similar fashion, declaring their wholehearted support for Parnell.

All in all, the family in which Joyce grew up shared a recalcitrant political and cultural temper, or what Joyce himself was later to call 'an inherited tenacity of heterodox resistance' (*u* 17.23). This showed in their laughter as much as their anger, and is written all over Joyce's work. The resistance was actually twofold. Fenians were intransigent in their hostility to England. But they were also traditional enemies of the Catholic clergy. They well knew what

Joyce's father kept on telling his son and Joyce himself stressed in his work: historically, the Irish Catholic Church had repeatedly opted for the 'compromise bargain' with the British state, to quote Irish socialist James Connolly.[5] Connolly claimed that, from the arrival of the first invaders from Britain in the twelfth century to the fall of Parnell, the Catholic hierarchy had repeatedly proved to be the political accomplice of the British state in Ireland. Connolly was influential on the young James Joyce, and Joyce's fictional alter ego, the young Stephen Dedalus, makes Connolly's point in *Ulysses*. The fate of Parnell seemed sufficient illustration of Connolly's thesis. Indeed, Parnell himself had finally come to recognize a crucial Fenian truth: the story of his own career finally justified Fenian anti-clericalism, and not the efforts he had made himself to woo the Catholic Church.

In declaring his enmity to the two imperial masters in Ireland, the British state and the Catholic Church, together, as he does, in *Ulysses*, Stephen is effectively declaring his allegiance to Fenian tradition. This is more specifically evident in his friendship with Kevin Egan evoked in Chapter 2. Egan was based on the real-life Fenian exile Joseph Casey. While in Paris in late 1902 and early 1903, through connections of his father's, Joyce met up with Casey. He found him sympathetic company, and spent time with him. Michael Davitt described Casey as 'having a leaning toward dynamite and a decided taste for absinthe' (*JJ*, p. 125). Joyce gives both to Egan. More importantly, Casey had taken part in the rescue of the IRB men known as the Manchester Martyrs and the bombing of Clerkenwell prison in London, both in 1867. Stephen's recollection of the fictional version of Casey in *Ulysses* is significant. That Casey and what he represents are now disregarded in Ireland only add to the point. For Joyce as for his father, like Parnell, Fenianism was a trusty old stick with which to beat new political tendencies. When Ulster Protestant Deasy labels Stephen a Fenian in the second chapter of *Ulysses*, he is not exactly right. In particular, Stephen, like Joyce, is a pacifist. Nonetheless, Deasy is by no means barking up the wrong tree.

Obviously enough, there is a large gulf between the young Stephen Dedalus and the mature Joyce who started *Ulysses* a decade or so after the date on which the novel is set. It is equally obvious that Joyce's work does not express a categorical, still less a crass, antagonism to either England or Roman Catholicism as wholes. It was precisely the tendency to think (and frequently to excoriate) the whole without feeling for irony, complication, exception or nuance that Joyce distrusted in Irish republican and nationalist tradition. He admired and felt affection for many aspects of English life and culture, from its Catholic intellectuals (Newman) to its great rebel writers (Milton, Blake, Byron, Shelley) to English socialism. He repeatedly accused England of refusing to acknowledge its debts to Ireland, but he himself was well aware of what he owed to England. He knew that England had empowered as well as disempowered him. If he viewed the conduct of the Catholic Church in modern Ireland with hauteur if not contempt, his profound intellectual debts to Catholicism ran from Aquinas to Newman. One of the aspects of Anglo-Irish literature that most annoyed him was its tendency to write Catholicism out of the historical Irish picture. When he claimed to have a medieval rather than a modern mind, he was proclaiming his sense of identity with the great Catholic artists: Dante, Rabelais, the medieval architects and craftsmen. The model for the structural principles on which *Ulysses* is founded is medieval and Catholic, as for example in Dante's scheme for the *Paradiso* in the *Convivio*, or the architectonics of the Gothic cathedral. Catholicism, Joyce asserted, was an absurdity. But it was at least a coherent absurdity, and he was not about to abandon it for the incoherent absurdity that was Protestantism.

Yet even granted great complexity of attitude, Joyce's heterodoxy is beyond any serious question. His radicalism, his opposition to the politics of the two *imperia* and the cultural formations on which they pervasively left their mark, poke up irrepressibly from every nook and cranny of his work. Indeed, the point is not only that Joyce's aesthetic practice owed a considerable debt to Fenianism and Parnellism together. As a result of his vast success, Joycean heterodoxy also became a cornerstone of modernism; which means that modernism itself owes a debt to Parnellism and Fenianism, and their will to resist British rule.

3

Youth in Nineties Dublin

In the first chapter of *A Portrait*, Joyce recalls the return of Parnell's coffin to Dublin, and the sorrowing mass of people who turned out to greet it, with an elegiac intensity that adolescence and young manhood seem to have done little to mute. In the second chapter, the young Stephen Dedalus has to remind himself that it is indeed Parnell and not he himself who has died. The shock of the loss of Parnell, its lasting significance, could hardly be more poignantly evoked. The Irish had dubbed Parnell the Chief, or Ireland's Uncrowned King. Though not himself of Catholic stock, he had come to incarnate the Irish redeemer, the Moses who would lead his people from captivity. Catholic Ireland had dreamed of this mythical figure since the colonial iniquities of the eighteenth century and before. Not surprisingly, Parnell's death spelled the end of Irish political hopes and a chronic slump in political morale. Parnell's party fell to squabbling with itself. Fenianism was at a low ebb and likewise splintering into factions. New eventualities in Irish politics – Connolly and Irish socialism, Arthur Griffith and Sinn Féin – were still some years away. Though it has a very specific focus, Joyce's short story 'Ivy Day in the Committee Room' aptly captures the mood of the times. The group of characters who feature in it may be rather feebly nostalgic for the days of Parnell. But they are involved in a shabby municipal election, and concerns like the canvasser's reward (free beer) loom equally large in their minds. Joyce pointedly seats them round a cindery, whitening fire.

According to W. B. Yeats, 'the modern literature of Ireland' began precisely with Parnell's fall from grace. A 'disillusioned and embittered' nation turned away from parliamentary politics and invested its creative energies in culture.[6] Certainly, the 1890s saw an explosion of cultural activity. To understand it, however, we must retrace our historical steps. From the late eighteenth century, Irish scholars – meaning scholars from the Protestant gentry; if one excepts the Catholic poet James Clarence Mangan, whom Joyce consciously took as his Irish literary forebear, there were no others – had done an increasing amount of research on ancient Ireland. The culmination of all this work was Standish O'Grady's *History of Ireland: Heroic Period* (1878–81). O'Grady's *History* was enormously influential. It was published just before Joyce was born. It was the most crucial work of Irish historiography of the period. However, it was not a product of what O'Grady called 'the labours of the patient brood of scholars'.[7] O'Grady was concerned with the heroic, pre-Christian age in Ireland. His sources were mythological as much as they were historical: legends, sagas, 'bardic story'.[8] In Lady (Augusta) Gregory's phrase, this kind of historical writing did not 'go bail for the facts'.[9]

O'Grady's *History* was enormously influential. It was the founding text of what became known as the Revival. Understanding something of the Revival is very important for understanding Joyce and his work, above all, *A Portrait of the Artist as a Young Man*. The Revival was quite a diverse phenomenon, and the movements and groups it spawned were also diverse. Its effects were felt beyond Dublin and indeed beyond Ireland, notably in the Irish community in London. But there were two aspects of revivalism that were particularly significant for Joyce. On the one hand, Gaelic revivalists like Douglas Hyde, Eoin MacNeill and Patrick Pearse were bent on reawakening a host of suppressed, forgotten or buried features of Irish culture and tradition: Irish games, Irish pastimes, the Irish language itself. If Ireland after Parnell was not to gain political independence, it could at least assert its own authentic cultural identity. The 1880s and '90s saw the appearance of organizations like the Celtic Literary Society, the Gaelic League, the Gaelic Athletic Association and the 'Daughters of Ireland'. In the '90s, at least, such organizations explicitly put culture before politics and even stood apart from politics.

On the other hand, the '90s also witnessed the birth of the Anglo-Irish Literary Revival. This was chiefly represented in the figures of W. B. Yeats, George Moore, Lady Gregory, Edward Martyn, J. M. Synge and George Russell, also known as AE. Joyce has sometimes been identified with them. But unlike most of the leading Gaelic revivalists, these were Anglo-Irishmen and women who, like the earlier scholars, tended to come of Ascendancy stock and were largely scions of landowning or wealthy families. Most of them were descendants of the 'strangers', the comparatively small group of British invaders who (in Joyce's terms) had none the less succeeded in historically subduing and dominating Ireland. The difference between them and the Catholic or 'Celtic' Irish was often cast as racial, and sometimes still is. But what was supremely at issue was class. What set Joyce and the Catholic Irish at odds with the Anglo-Irish were long-lived, indurated and ferocious questions of class difference, power and powerlessness, possession and dispossession, differences between the two kinds of Irish that were both economic and profoundly cultural.

By the 1890s, however, the Anglo-Irish were obviously playing a historical endgame. It had been increasingly clear since O'Connell that, with the exception of Ulster, the power of the Catholic majority in Ireland was steadily waxing and would lead at length to some form of independence. The power of the Irish ruling class had correspondingly waned. Parnell had seen that: that was partly why he had declared himself on the side of Catholic Ireland. Licensed by Parnell's example, the Anglo-Irish Revival was a last-ditch attempt to substitute cultural for political and economic power. The Anglo-

Irish revivalists hoped to attach themselves more securely to the country that appeared to be slipping from their grasp. They aimed at cultural unity or syncretism, the 'fusion of cultures' for which Yeats worked.[10] They strove to find a common ground between the Anglo-Irish and Gaelic worlds. The trouble was that the dream of fusion was quite extraordinarily remote from reality. The reality was pervasive division. As in so many colonial cultures, power in Ireland thrived on the fundamental inequities it had established. This had generated deep-rooted splits and conflicts. Furthermore, the Anglo-Irish revivalists more or less tacitly assumed that their class background, education and privileged social position entitled them to play the leading role in the new Irish culture. Catholics and nationalists were not about to let them do that, even if it meant getting a bad press from subsequent historians.

Joyce blatantly dissented from the more familiar nationalist expressions of displeasure with the Anglo-Irish Revival. He was very responsive to some of the art it produced. He knew that Yeats in particular was writing poetry of exquisite beauty, albeit a beauty to whose emotional mainsprings the poet himself did not give an altogether direct expression. When, in 1899, a nationalist audience greeted a performance of Yeats's great play *The Countess Cathleen* with boos and hisses, Joyce was one of the few who defiantly clapped it. But he was also to recognize that he was involved in a fight with the Anglo-Irish over terrain that was political as well as cultural, where the future of Ireland was quite as much at stake as its past. 'Will they wrest from us, from me, the palm of beauty?' muses Stephen Dedalus, during a confrontation with a group of literary revivalists in *Ulysses* (*u* 9.740). Joyce's answer, like Stephen's, was evidently no. As things turned out, he was to mount a challenge to the Anglo-Irish revivalist project that was quite beyond the conception of those who booed Yeats's play.

Political schism and stagnation, decline and despair in the wake of Parnell, the rise of Irish cultural nationalism as exemplified in the Gaelic Revival, the cultural 'last stand' of the Anglo-Irish: these were the three most important features of the culture in which Joyce grew into adolescence. They affected his early life in ways small and large, psychological, intellectual and practical. On the one hand, the Joyce family fortunes went from bad to worse, as did John Stanislaus's habits and health. He had to sell off his Cork property and, for a while, moved the family to the lower-class area of Drumcondra (where, significantly, Stephen would later assert that 'they speak the best English', *P*, p. 193). At one drunken moment, John Stanislaus tried to strangle his wife, exclaiming, 'Now, by God, is the time to finish it!' (*JJ*, p. 41). James's schooling did not suffer, however. After a brief interlude at a Christian Brothers' school – with 'Paddy Stink and Micky Mud' (*JJ*, p. 35), as his father uncharitably put it – he was enrolled at Belvedere College. The Jesuit education he received there was close in quality to the one provided at Clongowes. Among other things, it gave him an excellent grasp of some of the languages (Latin, French, Italian) that were later to prove so important to him.

James remained loyal to Parnell, too, even when the Parnellite cause had long been lost. In the early 1890s, he had written a poem entitled 'Et tu, Healy?' denouncing what he took to be the treachery of Parnell's sometime lieutenant. As late as 1897 he was wearing an ivy leaf on his collar on 6 October, the date of Parnell's death. Stephen's solitary, obstinate defence of Byron against the charge of being 'a bad man' in *A Portrait* (*P*, p. 83) was modelled on an instance in Joyce's life. This had its roots in a conviction that Joyce derived from the fate of Parnell: Irish Catholicism shared with Victorian England a puritanical and repressive morality in matters sexual. Irish nationalism shared it, too. The Anglo-Irish revivalists were scarcely less prissy. As he put it himself, they were happy to dream their dreamy dreams, leaving him to be the sewer that carried off their filthy streams. The sexual morality of Victorian England and Ireland was not only psychologically and artistically but politically destructive. Certainly, Joyce himself was quick to resist it, losing his virginity at the age of fourteen to a prostitute he met on the canal bank. His sexual interests placed him at a distance from genteel Dublin culture, to which he nonetheless remained tied through his connections to the household of the MP David Sheehy, of which more later. Sex also got him into trouble, not least with the Jesuit authorities at Belvedere, where the rector described him as 'inclined to evil ways' (*JJ*, p. 48). Joyce repented, mortified himself, surrendered once more. This time, he knew: there was no way back. He and his work would become notorious for their sexual extravagance. This had its origins in his unstinting determination to flout the prudery of the culture in which he grew up. Here, again, Joyce was Parnellite in his obduracy. He was not going to have his sexuality cowed by the two imperial masters.

Parnell's ghost – the ghost of the leader who had coolly taken the colonizer on at his own game – also haunted the young James Joyce's adolescent demeanour. He 'constructed the enigma of a manner' (*SH*, p. 27), cultivating a studied hauteur, a silent detachment and seeming indifference to the world around him. This was partly a defence against the pain of the tawdry life his father had inflicted on the family, and from which he 'suffered greatly' (*SH*, p. 29). But, the young Joyce's intellectual aloofness was also a Parnellite gesture turned on a culture that he stubbornly continued to see as having betrayed Parnell, and therefore Ireland itself. This is a crucial reason for his pronounced lack of sympathy for the Gaelic Revival. Beneath the most vigorous assertions of so-called Irishness – the emphasis on health and fitness, for example, or the military spirit of the Gaelic Athletic Association – Joyce's preternaturally acute sense of irony detected, not only a slavish obedience to the Church, but a continuing subservience to contemporary English cultural models. This was true, not least, of the emergence of cultural nationalism itself, which was an English before it was an Irish phenomenon. Thus, in *A Portrait*, Stephen emphatically repudiates the 'hollow-sounding voices' of his schoolmasters, the patriots and nationalists together, urging him to be a good Catholic, 'strong, manly and healthy' and true to his country (*p*, p. 86). The Gaelic Revival seemed to deny what the young Joyce everywhere treasured: 'speculation', 'hardihood of thought', 'an independence of the soul' (*sh*, p. 77, 100, 111). These in themselves were aesthetic and intellectual versions of the great Parnellite virtues. Indeed, a culture more capable of exercising them would never have abandoned Parnell or its own political cause.

In the 1890s, however, Joyce was by no means so distant from the Anglo-Irish Revival. This was hardly surprising: in the figure of Yeats, at least, it was producing the best English poetry of the decade. Joyce's first collection of poems, now lost, had the eminently Yeatsian title, *Moods*. Indeed, the young Joyce was very much caught up in moods, particularly melancholy ones. He adopted the melancholia dominant in so much revivalist verse of the '90s (though he gave it his own distinctive inflection). *A Portrait* tells us a great deal about this. In Chapter 2, for example, Stephen Dedalus seems well on the way to becoming one of what Yeats called 'the children of revery', 'feeble and worn', with 'griefstruck face'.[11] Joyce also shared a specifically Parnellite melancholia of the '90s which itself was in large measure Revival-derived. The revivalists were much more imaginatively engaged by the dead Parnell than they had been by the living one. In effect, they were haunted by what Yeats called 'the shade of Parnell' (*cw*, p. 191).[12]

The Anglo-Irish revivalists did not just go in for protracted meditations on the Irish past. They were learned and steeped in literature. Joyce set out to emulate them, reading avidly, and astonishingly widely. Where Catholic nationalism tended to follow the Church in being suspicious of when not actually hostile to 'modernity', the revivalists were interested in the most recent literary trends, not least European ones. Joyce followed suit, most conspicuously, in his love of Ibsen, the great truth-telling genius of another small,

A child of revery:
Althea Gyles's
proposed binding
design for Yeats's
*The Wind Among
the Reeds* (1899).

modern nation emerging on the edge of Europe and about to free
itself from foreign domination. Yeats and his allies were genuinely
and passionately ambitious, not just for themselves, but for
what they took to be Irish culture. They wanted to create a great
European literature in English. That was their conception of a
modern Irish literature. Joyce shared their ambition, but on behalf
of an Ireland quite unlike the Ireland cherished by the Anglo-Irish.
He would massively fulfil this ambition, to a degree that even Yeats
himself could not.

4

An Intellectual Young Man, 1898–1903

The years 1898–1903 formed a distinct and very significant stage in the emergence of modern Ireland. The period is bounded by two major pieces of legislation, the Local Government Act of 1898 and Wyndham's Land Act of 1903. These marked what was virtually a peaceful revolution. The end of the Gladstone government in 1895 had dealt the final blow to all hopes of Home Rule. But the advent of a Conservative–Unionist government was by no means the disaster that some Irish might have feared. For the Conservatives now spoke of the need to 'kill Home Rule with kindness'.[13] The new, conciliatory attitude produced what became known as 'constructive Unionism'. It bred policies that were more reformist than not, and led to some progressive changes.

The Local Government Act was one example of this: it set up county and district councils to which Catholics as well as Protestants could be elected. Substantial numbers of the Catholic Irish – not least, Irishwomen – could now be appointed to positions of power and responsibility in local government. In effect, the Act transferred the governing power in local affairs from the Unionists to the Nationalists. After 1898, control over a range of administrative bodies passed from the hands of a Protestant elite to the very largely Catholic democracy. Local government might seem like a footling, petit bourgeois, basely unmodernist concern. But it was Yeats who felt contempt for the Irish petit bourgeois fumbling 'in a greasy till'.[14] Joyce was happy to fumble, and hardly averse to grease or tills. He had, he said, 'a grocer's assistant's mind' (*JJ*, p. 28). He filled *Ulysses* with characters from the Dublin lower middle class. He turned an advertising canvasser into the great modern hero and calculated his character's budget for 16 June 1904 with meticulous if problematic care. The Land Act was less directly significant for Dublin, but was immensely significant for Ireland as a whole. It allowed and encouraged Irish tenants to buy out their landlords, aided by Treasury loans. It pointed to the end, not only of the gross injustice of land distribution in colonial Ireland, but of the violence and disorder to which that injustice had repeatedly given rise. Once again, the new legislation marked a decisive gain in power for Catholics, at least, in rural Ireland, at the expense of the Anglo-Irish.

Between 1898 and 1903, then, the political status of the Irish Catholic classes changed quite markedly. The classes in question were those to which Joyce belonged and with whom, even at his most critical, he always in some sense identified. Indeed he was to give them their great work of modern genius, as Ibsen had given the Norwegians theirs. When Stephen finally declares, in *A Portrait*, that he is determined 'to forge in the smithy of my soul the uncreated conscience of my race' (*P*, p. 257), he is committing himself to doing precisely what Joyce understood Ibsen to have done. But if Irish Catholics found themselves newly empowered, it was only by virtue of English condescension and within the limits of continuing English domination. 'Constructive unionism' was hand-me-down. The benefits it conferred were what Joyce would later call the 'orts and offals' from a rich man's table (*U* 9.1094–5). The Local Government and Land Acts had not emerged from an Irish parliament. There had been no such body since 1800, when it had closed down before the Act of Union took effect. Nor had the Irish wrested their new powers from their overlords through sheer strength of political will, as Parnell had insisted that they should. The Ireland that was awakening with the dawn of the new century was also an

Ireland that remained subdued. For Joyce, it was therefore still an Ireland in darkness. He was to wrestle with this problem from many different angles.

At the turn of the century, there are two particularly important examples of what Joyce took to be the drag on Irish modernity. As Irish Catholics were increasingly empowered, new voices started to make themselves heard. In 1900, for example, D. P. Moran founded *The Leader*. Both he and his journal were roundly scathing about nationalism and revivalism in all their aspects. Moran thought the Irish were so far sunk in their enslavement that there was little or no hope of their redemption. His sensibility was modern, demotic, journalistic, harsh. There was an invigorating if rasping vitality to his prose at its best. Moran was impatient with what he thought of as Irish backwardness, subservience and complicity with England. Joyce undoubtedly learnt from him. But he did not share Moran's nativist promotion of an Irish Ireland, his blanket dismissal of Irish literature in English or the sometimes hysterical virulence of his animus against the Anglo-Irish revivalists. Most of all, he detested the racism and, in particular, the anti-Semitism into which Moran's emphasis on Irish purity sometimes tipped him.

So, too, with Arthur Griffith: between 1898 and 1904 Griffith was a 'coming man', at least, according to the central character in *Ulysses*, Leopold Bloom (*u* 18.386). He had long been active in the IRB, and had fought on what all good Irish nationalists took to be the right side in the Boer War (the Boers). In 1899 he took over the editorship of the *United Irishman*. He was to go on to found Sinn Féin (1906) and become the first President of the Irish Free State (1922). In the early years of the century, Joyce thought that the *United Irishman* was the only newspaper of any merit in Ireland. He approved of Griffith, Sinn Féin and their policies, as was logical enough, given his and his father's Parnellism and his family's Fenian connections. He thought Sinn Féin's project for an economic boycott of England 'the highest form of warfare I have heard of', not least because it was a form of non-violent resistance (*JJ*, pp. 237–8).

But given Boer attitudes to black Africans, Griffith's pro-Boerism also gave the game away. His political attitudes were both enlightened and benighted at once. The benightedness, again, emerged in matters of race. Leading figures in nineteenth-century Irish nationalism had repeatedly identified the predicament of the Irish with that of other races under British rule. There was also a pro-Jewish tradition in Irish nationalism that ran from Wolfe Tone through O'Connell to Michael Davitt. But Griffith identified Irish Jews as invaders, and therefore like the colonizer. He accused them of 'grinding' the poor and of conspiring with the English.[15] Some Irish nationalists of the early twentieth century resisted any call for racial or cultural purity. But with Griffith, if nationalism took another step forwards, it also took a big step back. Later, in *Ulysses*, Joyce would rebuke what he took to be the ignoble tendencies in nationalism. Joyce partly identified xenophobia, or what he called 'stranger-hating', with the British (*CW*, p. 16). Indeed, at this very time, the British were declaiming against 'undesirable aliens', a category which largely included Jews.[16] But that Irish nationalists' suspicion of racial outsiders came partly from the colonizer did not justify their continuing adherence to it. It merely deepened their implication in his habits of thought.

Joyce's various self-portraits suggest a young man whose character or cast of mind had several markedly different, dominant features. One constant is the emphasis on intellect. If 1898 was a momentous year for Catholic Ireland, it was also the year in which Joyce started at University College, Dublin. The provision of Catholic higher education in Ireland had traditionally been poor. In 1854 Newman had founded a Catholic university specifically for the Irish Catholic community. But it had languished, because it had no royal charter that would allow it to award degrees. It picked up momentum in the 1880s, however, once the Jesuits took it over and

University College,
St Stephen's Green,
Dublin, *c.* 1900.

it became part of the Royal University. By 1898, it was a thriving institution. The new political dispensation much enhanced its sense of its own importance. The generation of students to which Joyce belonged could expect to feature more prominently in Irish society and culture, to have more political power and higher social status than any generation preceding it. Not surprisingly, in the years when Joyce was a student there, it was a confident and lively institution. It was also politically vibrant, the dominant politics being nationalist.

Intellect is a resonant word in Joyce's writings. Again, this may partly have had something to do with Parnell, whom Gladstone had called 'an intellectual phenomenon' (*cw*, p. 338). But the young Joyce at University College also understood himself to be that strange, new, special creature, a modern, dissident, Irish Catholic intellectual. He was modern and dissident, of course, in proudly proclaiming the loss of his faith. He was offhandedly, disdainfully blasphemous, because he saw very well that a great deal of popular Catholic belief was merely childish: 'It's absurd: it's Barnum. He comes into the world God knows how, walks on the water, gets out of his grave and goes up off the Hill of Howth. What drivel is this?' (*sh*, p. 133). What thrills Joyce at such moments is Stephen's tone, the triumphant, modern sharpness that comes of having liberated oneself from obscurantism. In *Stephen Hero*, Stephen identifies his modernity with the 'vivisective' spirit which needs no lantern to guide it, but 'examines its territory by the light of day' (*SH*, p. 186). His dissidence shows in his rejection of 'the spiritual authorities of Catholicism and patriotism' together, the joint repudiation of 'the temporal authorities of the hierarchy and the government' (*SH*, pp. 172–3). Since he is a modern dissident, he commits himself to the labour of discovering a truth of his own, by means of his own intellect. This truth will have no prior foundation in dogma, precedent, tradition or an established body of knowledge. For Joyce as for Stephen, this was what being a modern intellectual meant. As a modern intellectual, he also saw himself, not only as a new event in Irish Catholic culture, but even as setting it an example. For he was exercising a will to autonomy as, for all its talk of independence, his culture did not dare to. '*Non serviam!*', declares Stephen ('I will not serve', *U* 15.4228). It is perhaps his most significant phrase.

Joyce was caught up in the spirit of radical change in Catholic Ireland from 1898 to 1903. But he also doubled and redoubled that spirit, radicalizing himself in manner that was quite beyond the imagination and comprehension of his contemporaries. He presented Catholic Ireland with an image of freedom that would comprehensively outstrip it for decades to come. Yet even for Joyce, freedom was always an extremely difficult concept, always a work in progress. In *Ulysses*, Stephen taps his forehead and declares that 'in here it is I must kill the priest and the king' (*U* 15.4436–37). But this is a young man's assertion. The older Joyce got, the more aware he became of the ironical limits to such a project. Not only did he recognize that authority reasserts its grip in the very work that seeks to loosen it. He understood the need to have it do so. If the young Joyce was a modern intellectual, he none the less also remained a Catholic intellectual if not a believer. He was a Catholic intellectual because of his background, education and class, because of the culture to which he did not cease to belong, just by virtue of dissenting from it. But he also consciously identified with Catholic intellect as exemplified in aspects of Catholic theological tradition. The chief sources, for example, of the aesthetic theory which he developed, and which is so significant a marker of Stephen's intellectual calibre, are Aquinas and Aristotle, the second, in large part, because of the Aristoteleanism of the first. The modern James Joyce may have vigorously resisted the oppressive power of Catholic tradition. But there was another Joyce who asserted his allegiance to that tradition, and never left it, or wanted to leave it, behind him.

5

The Artist as Critic

This same period saw Joyce's appearance as a literary critic. The fact is important for two reasons. First, from his adolescence onwards, Joyce had been producing poems, plays in prose and verse and 'epiphanies'. But he emerged as a critic before he could properly deem himself to have embarked on a literary career. As a modern, dissident, Irish Catholic intellectual, he was thinking about literature before he had committed any very significant literature to paper. Second, to a remarkable extent, his essays, reviews and lectures form a coherent but evolving body of work around a specific and focused set of concerns. Joyce's non-fictional prose is therefore worth consideration as a whole. Whatever their other concerns – art's power, for instance – the critical writings repeatedly turn out to be about Ireland, its history and prospects, its politics and culture, its relation to the Church and the colonial power and, perhaps above all, the place of art in the Ireland Joyce knew. They address these themes deftly, if sometimes indirectly, by way of metaphor, analogy, allegory. Even when Joyce is review-ing a trifling book or commenting on what seems to be an insignificant piece of public business, he is reflecting on contem-porary Ireland, and his own position in it. Thus a review of Alfred Ainger's book on Crabbe becomes a meditation on the squalor and 'inevitable moral decay' of British life at a distance from the centres of power (cw, p. 90). Equally, Jacques Lebaudy's mis-adventures in the Sahara inspire an ironical account of imperialist

Mihály Munkácsy, *Ecce Homo*, 1895–6, oil on canvas.

practice, especially the 'capable management' of the British
Empire (*cw*, p. 100).

Joyce's first five significant essays and reviews are indicative.
One of his earliest forays into criticism was an account of Mihály
Munkácsy's painting 'Ecce Homo', which was exhibited in Dublin
in 1899. The essay makes full sense only if we appreciate how far
it is a political allegory. Munkácsy was Hungarian. Irish nationalists
had been comparing the Irish with the Hungarian political situation since 1848. Hungary and Ireland were both countries at the
wings of Europe. Both were struggling their arduous way towards
independence and political modernity in opposition to a dominant, imperial power. Joyce's essay is a mordantly sceptical
rewriting of the Irish–Hungarian analogy from the standpoint
of a disabused Parnellite. Munkácsy's Christ before Pilate is an
allegory of Parnell before the bar of English public opinion. He
has Parnell's 'endurance, passion . . . and dauntless will'. But the
redeemer has been abandoned by his people, who display only
'the fire of rejection, the bitter unwisdom of their race'. Not surprisingly, the representatives of the Empire, the imperial Roman

soldiery, observe the dismal spectacle with 'self-possessed contempt' (*CW*, p. 20).

'Drama and Life' is Joyce's first essay on Ibsen. It offers an account of the relationship between art, specifically drama, and the self-assertion of a race entering into the fullness of its power. The early theatre of emergent races characteristically draws on myths. These provide the material for national self-expression, though they differ with different people and times. This cultural formation is perceptible in modern Norway and Germany (and, by implication, Ireland) as it once was in ancient Greece and old England. 'Ibsen's New Drama' is about *When We Dead Awaken*. Joyce reads the play as concerned with the 'soul-crises' of a people coming to modern consciousness (*CW*, p. 31). Here, again, his Ibsen is a Norwegian version of Parnell. Ibsen mounts a 'plan of campaign' (*CW*, p. 30). When it provokes a storm of protest, like

Henrik Ibsen: Joyce wrote of his 'admiration at the gradual, irresistible advance of this extraordinary man' ('Ibsen's New Drama', *CW*, p. 13).

Parnell, he coolly holds the kerfuffle at a distance. For he is obstinately intent on sustaining his own distinctive vision of modern Norway. In Ibsen, a new, modern, national art triumphs over the insidiously retrograde forces that he dramatizes in his characters.

But alas, so far, Ireland has not produced its Ibsen. This is clear from 'The Day of the Rabblement'. In Ireland, the Irish Literary Theatre has failed to expel 'the old devil' (*cw*, p. 50). It has rather capitulated to 'the rabblement of the most belated race in Europe', by which Joyce means the race that has proved to be the most reluctant to face the challenge of modernity, if for historical reasons. In comparison with Ibsen, the trouble with Irish artists is their persistence in servitude. They are unable to break with and even willingly connive in their own subjugation. They 'inherit a will broken by doubt and a soul that yields up all its hate to a caress' (*cw*, p. 52). This too was Mangan's predicament. In 'James Clarence Mangan', Joyce writes tenderly of Mangan's 'vastation of soul' (*cw*, p. 58). But for all his defiance of colonial 'injustice', Mangan cannot get beyond 'noble misery'. His tradition 'is so much with him', writes Joyce, that 'he has accepted it with all its griefs and failures, and has not known how to change it, as the strong spirit knows' (*cw*, pp. 58–9). Unlike Ibsen, Mangan submits, gives way. He yields to the traditions of a race that itself remains straitly enclosed by history. In doing so, he acquiesces in their defeat. He remains complicit with the conqueror, and finally lets his people down. Joyce will be invincibly determined to avoid this trap.

There are two particularly significant points in Joyce's development as a critic. The first came in 1902, when the editor of the Dublin *Daily Express*, E. V. Longworth, started to send him books to review. The *Express* had had an interesting recent history. Traditionally a stuffily conservative publication, in 1898 it was taken over by Horace Plunkett and editor T. P. Gill. They promptly turned it in a liberal and nationalist direction. Most importantly of all, Gill instituted a literary supplement. This provided a forum for Yeats and other leading revivalists. Then, in 1899, in Yeats's phrase, the paper fell into the hands of 'the extreme Tory party'.[17] Its owner sold it to a syndicate headed by the Guinness magnate, Lord Ardilaun, and including the passionate Unionist and later Ulster leader Edward Carson. By 1903 it was generally thought of as a 'mouthpiece for Unionism'.[18] Thus the nationalist Miss Ivors teases Gabriel Conroy about reviewing for it in Joyce's story 'The Dead'. Certainly, a young 'fenian' reviewer like James Joyce had to watch his step.[19] For a time, he did so skilfully, and apparently imperturbably. His first review for Longworth, for example, excoriated the nationalist poet William Rooney as 'a weary and foolish spirit' (*cw*, p. 62). This must have seemed promising. Beneath the surface, however, Joyce was hardly pursuing a Unionist line. If Rooney's poetry was bad, he suggested, it was because, as nationalist poetry, it was insufficiently ambitious, still too much the poetry of a colonial subject. It precisely lacked the Ibsenite (and Joycean) will to independence. There was no piece in the book that had 'the quality of integrity, the quality of being separate and whole' (*cw*, p. 62).

Writing for a conservative organ like the *Express* required adroitness and cunning. Joyce adopted a wry, watchful, detached, sometimes rather lofty critical manner, seldom breaking into the open from a delicately ironical cover. This manner, however, concealed a clandestine intellectual agenda that was aesthetic and political together. The double strategy of the Rooney review became typical. But it was not just a consequence of Joyce's undoubted political shrewdness. Irony was the logical product of a genuine political ambivalence. The *Express* reviews quietly but repeatedly debunk both the classes and the values to which the *Express* was most committed. 'An Effort at Precision in Thinking', for example, is tersely dismissive of James Anstie's sheltered, genteel conception of what 'common people' might be (*cw*, p. 69). This is less than surprising: Anstie was chaplain-in-ordinary to Queen Victoria. 'Colonial Verses' is similarly dismissive of the fulsome, servile self-abasement of loyalist Canadian poet Clive Phillips-Wolley. More interestingly and significantly, 'George Meredith' reads Meredith, a radical liberal but also a sentimental Celticist and Unionist, not as a novelist but as a philosophical essayist. This is partly an ironical gibe at the insubstantiality of Meredith's fictional world, its lack of historical density. But Joyce also calls Meredith a man of letters, specifically not an 'epical artist' (*cw*, p. 64). The first was precisely what he himself was striving not to be. The second was what he would finally become.

But it is the Anglo-Irish revivalists at whom the larger part of the young Joyce's salvos are aimed. 'Today and Tomorrow in Ireland', for example, deftly rebukes the callowness of most revivalist poetry. Insofar as it touches on colonialism, 'New Fiction' is about colonial India rather than Ireland, but that does not stop Joyce taking potshots at the occultist interests of the modern descendants of Irish colonizers. He engaged in this kind of sniping because he was acutely aware that the intellectual distinction of the bulk of most revivalist work was in inverse proportion to the social distinction of the individuals responsible for it. He mocked the triviality or sheer intellectual nullity of minor Anglo-Irish revivalists, scholars and writers: Arnold Graves, Robert Tyrrell, Albert Canning (second son of the first Baron Garvagh). After 1899, these were the kind of literary luminaries most appropriate to the *Express*. Joyce was no doubt aware of the fact, and handled them accordingly. But if he was happy to 'slate [their] drivel to Jaysus', he was quite as willing to treat much more eminent figures in the same way (*u* 9.1160). Most piquantly of all, Longworth had actually approached Joyce on the recommendation of Lady Gregory. In 'The Soul of Ireland', a review of her *Poets and Dreamers*, Joyce duly bit the hand of the aristocratic woman who had fed him. But Yeats, as he knew and explicitly stated in 'Today and Tomorrow in Ireland', was a superb exception.[20] As we will see later, he would learn to deal with Yeats quite differently.

If the Anglo-Irish Revival gets short shrift from the young Joyce, Catholic Ireland in general and nationalism in particular might seem to fare little better. But the critiques should not be confused, as though Joyce were indifferently calling down a plague on both houses. In any case, he does not so much develop a critique of nationalist tradition as admonish it. The admonition is itself two-pronged, with one line of thought following on from the Rooney and the other from the Mangan essay. On the one hand, says Joyce, unlike Parnell, present-day nationalism thinks too small. A nationalist like Stephen Gwynn is altogether too conciliatory. He may formulate a 'distinct accusation of English civilization'. But 'give Ireland the status of Canada and Mr Gwynn becomes an Imperialist at once' (*cw*, p. 55). In this, Gwynn is in fact exactly in harmony with the *Express* which, for all its conservatism, actually claimed that it sought to reconcile 'the rights and impulses of Irish nationality with the demands and obligations of imperial dominions'.[21] In pointing an obliquely satirical finger at Gwynn, Joyce was also pointing at the very paper for which he was writing. On the other hand, nationalist tradition also demonstrated its continuing subservience in another way. It seemed unable to let go of habits of rage, 'tears and lamentations', high-sounding but empty threats (*cw*, p. 67). This meant that it remained intensely bound up in its relationship with the historical victor. Ireland could apparently not stop paying tribute to its conqueror. In this respect, even as unlikely a colonized people as the Burmese, who preserved a 'serene and order-loving' national temper and refused 'to make the battlefield a test of excellence', might offer a lesson to Irish political culture (ibid.). Better Olympian indifference than implacable grief and resentment: indeed, 'A Peep into History' rises so coolly superior to the issues involved in the Popish Plot (for Irish nationalists, one of many classic historical points of reference) that it ends up almost identifying with the 'indecent levity' of Charles ii (*cw*, p. 84).

How much Longworth understood of Joyce's agenda as a reviewer is open to question. For a while, at least, the Rooney review may have allayed suspicion. But the technique of sly point-scoring finally struck home. Without consulting Joyce, Longworth tacked a sentence of praise for the binding and printing of Gwynn's book on to the end of Joyce's distinctly unenthusiastic account of it. This was a blatant bit of log-rolling, and Joyce did not forget it, or forgive Longworth for associating him with it. He waited ten months before taking his revenge. Then he responded in kind, damning the binding of a London-produced book as inconsequentially as Longworth had lauded the Dublin-produced one. Longworth promptly sacked him, and threatened to throw him downstairs if he ever came into the offices of the *Express* again. But to offend Longworth or damn the ugliness of an English book was hardly to mount a vigorous challenge to the British state and its culture. Joyce's reviews do not leave the Church unscathed: in 'Aristotle on Education', for example, he obliquely hints at the importance for a republican of clearly separating Church and state, and 'A French Religious Novel' praises a modern struggle with Catholic orthodoxy that is finally blighted by 'the horrible image of the Jansenist Christ' (*cw*, p. 86). But with the exception of 'Humanism', which might seem indirectly to treat the intellectual limitations of English pragmatism and common sense, there is comparatively little criticism of the other 'imperial master' per se. However, this lasted only as far as Trieste. Here, as we will see, as lecturer and journalist, Joyce would remedy the deficiency with a vengeance.

6

16 June 1904

I have made quite a lot of Joyce's assertion of himself specifically as an intellectual. He had good historical, political and cultural reasons for it. But we should not allow it to confuse us. Like that of other modernists, Joyce's work has been a godsend to academics. It is both erudite and obscure enough to justify endless research projects and attempts at explication and annotation. Joyce knew what he was doing. He was very well aware that it was the modern scholar who could best ensure the survival of his work. But pitching to the scholar had its downside. For modern academics have tended to turn him into their own mirror-image. The scholars' picture of Joyce has often been one of a writer absorbed in his researches. His ideal home would have been a major holding library. Alternatively, Joyce turns out to have been intent on an abstrusely theoretical project, on proving the truth of some mid- to late-twentieth-century intellectual paradigm. In either case, we get a detached, abstracted and notably passionless man, a man who lived by and for the mind.

In fact, Joyce led a life that was remarkably unlike that of most modern scholars, not least because it would make a complete mess of a career trajectory. It was in many respects a convulsive, tumultuous, impulsive life. Joyce fed off its very precariousness, the threat of total chaos that so often lay within it. This is clear from some of its most repetitive features: rows, fallings-out, fears and angsts, sexual giddiness, violent paranoias, fecklessness with money, scenes with landlords, debts. Joyce's (sometimes night-long) drinking bouts were a frequent feature of his life from Dublin through Trieste to Paris in the 1920s and '30s. Robert McAlmon remembered the two men waking to the raw light of a Paris dawn in a café at which they had been drinking all night. Looking at the floor, he saw that it was littered with the small cigars that had fallen unlit from their lips. With the exception of a few settled years in the Square Robiac in the mid- to late 1920s, the Joyce family led a life of constant upheaval. This was only aggravated in the '30s, as they scurried haplessly about Europe in an agonized search for a solution to the problem of daughter Lucia's schizophrenia.

Scholars have not always ignored Joyce's more extravagant side. But they have tended to treat it in relation to the demands of his work. If his work exacted an enormous toll, however, then so did his lifestyle, not least on his health. Joyce provided his own account of the psychic economy he took to be at stake: he had, he said, equal and opposite powers of abandonment and recuperation. But what we know of his life tells us something more significant than that. For the accounts of a Joyce repeatedly brought home in the early hours of the morning looking like a limp rag-doll bear witness in reverse, not just to his tenacity, but to the sheer ardour of his sense of purpose. Nothing short of pure and incandescent will could have kept him going at all. Nothing else could have kept him writing novels, let alone *Ulysses* and *Finnegans Wake*. His emotional life may have had two aspects; it also had a single logic. The intensity with which he lived was also the intensity with which he thought and wrote about Ireland. There was one particular figure who was the focus for this intensity in practically all its forms. That figure was Nora. Joyce said he loved no one apart from his family. Of his family, he loved no member as much as he did her.

Joyce set *Ulysses* in Dublin on a single day, 16 June 1904. In doing so, he almost certainly commemorated the date on which he first walked out with Nora Barnacle. Joyce wrote of Blake that, 'like many other men of genius', he 'was not attracted by cultivated and refined women' (*cw*, p. 177). He would have said the same of himself. Whilst he liked the company of educated and intellectual women, with the occasional exception, his emotional needs and sexual tastes largely pointed him elsewhere. In their different ways, both *Stephen Hero* and *A Portrait of the Artist as a Young* Man chart a process of alienation from contained, respectable, genteel, young Dublin womanhood. Stephen is by no means immune to the loveliness of Emma. In this he mirrors Joyce's own responsiveness to his adolescent love Mary (though Emma is not a fictional version of her). Mary was the daughter of upwardly mobile David Sheehy MP, who was then in the process of transforming himself from troublesome IRB man into what his grandson Conor Cruise O'Brien would later call 'a respectable, Victorian Catholic' paterfamilias.[22] Not surprisingly, perhaps, Emma is finally a reason for despair. Both Joyce and Stephen regretfully draw away from her streak of middle-class prudence, of self-intent reserve. For all the pride of her young flesh, she is simply too 'sensible' (*sh*, p. 197). When, at the end of 'Grace' in *Dubliners*, Father Purdon declares himself to be the 'spiritual accountant' of 'business men' (*d*, p. 174), he demonstrates just how far his creator was inclined to associate Emma's kind of calculation with the contemporary Irish Catholic Church. Joyce also identified it with English petit bourgeois culture and its economic fetish. So much is clear when, in *Ulysses*, Ulsterman Deasy asserts the value of a cardinal English principle: what is the Englishman's 'proudest boast? *I paid my way*' (*u* 2.251).

In contrast to both these forces, Nora brought Joyce Ireland, or at least, Ireland beyond the Pale. 'Thirty miles outside Dublin and I am lost', Joyce once said.[23] That was where Nora took over. Nora came from Galway, in the west of Ireland. The west, of course, was a world apart from Dublin, a backward world of landlords and peasantry where Gaelic was still spoken. It had suffered and was still suffering from the grim legacies of famine and emigration. Nonetheless, it was now also attracting the romantic attentions of

High Street, Galway,
c. 1901.

the *littérateurs*, particularly Yeats, Synge and Lady Gregory. Not
that Galway was rural Ireland: it was a city with a history and
ambitions, though also an impoverished one. Nora's ambivalent
symbolism – western and urban at the same time – was enormously
significant for Joyce.

Nora's father was a baker, her mother a seamstress. She left
school at the age of twelve. When her uncle beat her for consorting
with a Protestant boy, she fled home for Dublin, where she worked
as a chambermaid in Finn's (now legendary) Hotel. Nora was neither respectable nor middle-class nor contained. In the phrase of
her excellent biographer, she was 'a Catholic girl without a Catholic
conscience'.[24] Like some of the women who appear in Joyce's
novels, she was pure and brazen at once. It was a mixture that
Joyce responded to very intensely. He was later to pay tribute to
her as 'a simple, honourable soul'.[25] But simple did not mean naïve.
Piquantly for the modernist calendar, she probably put her hand
inside Joyce's trousers and jerked him off on their first date. For
Joyce, however, Nora's shamelessness was not at all incompatible

with what he called her nobility. Indeed, the two went hand in hand. At all events, Nora fell passionately in love with him, as, shortly after, he did with her.

Living on the edge of chaos meant putting oneself at the mercy of chance. But Joyce thrived on accidents. He particularly liked them when they seemed to be pregnant with meaning or to fit into a pattern. He partly built *Ulysses* and *Finnegans Wake* like a *bricoleur*, putting hosts of incidental little finds in useful places within a massively coherent structure. The errors of genius 'are volitional', says Stephen in *Ulysses*, 'and are the portals of discovery' (*U* 9.229). For Joyce, accidents led to discoveries too. Some of the most crucial events in his life may seem like ordinary, human, random occurrences. Yet it is hard not to think of them as also fraught with symbolic value, as though the artist's will had prevailed from the start. His encounter with Nora is an obvious example. Joyce's fortunes were at a low ebb. In late 1902 he had forsaken Dublin for Paris, supposing that he would be able to study and write with greater freedom there. He had been summoned back home in April 1903 by the news that his mother was dying, though in fact she lasted until August. With his mother gone, his father's morale had plummeted even further. The family was in crisis, and its prospects looked bleak.

Joyce was more and more inclined to think that Ireland's did, too. His alienation from established Irish politics, the Revival and the Irish literary scene in general had progressively deepened. The leading revivalists had at best patronized him (though they had also sometimes lent him money). George Russell had excluded him from a new anthology of young Irish poets. Meanwhile, the Irish Parliamentary Party slipped from one venal political expedient to another. Certainly, 'constructive Unionism' was producing some results. But 'constructive Unionism' spelt patronage not liberation. The foundation of Sinn Féin was still a few years off. Not surprisingly, perhaps, given his own and his family's economic circumstances,

Joyce was drawn to the socialist politics then gaining momentum in Britain and spreading to Ireland. The early years of the British Labour movement were actually much more important to and influential on Joyce than Marx was, and he shared some of its unpretentious radicalism, though he was no doubt wary of its often dismayingly superior attitude to the Irish. He briefly interested himself in James Connolly's Irish Republican Socialist Party.[26] But he had regretfully to admit that socialism was unlikely to gain a hold in Ireland. Outside Ulster, Ireland had very little by way of an industrial working-class. Indeed, like other aspects of Irish modernity, and like the conscience of the race, the Irish proletariat had still to be created.

In the first three chapters of *Ulysses*, Joyce quite precisely evokes both his own real-life dilemma and his symbolic predicament in 1904. He places Stephen in one of the Martello Towers that ring the coast of Ireland. William Pitt had these built in 1804, as a defence against a French invasion. To many Irish, they were symbols of colonial domination. Stephen has two companions. Both can see that he is what he will later call Shakespeare, a man of 'unremitting intellect' and 'a lord of language' (*U* 9.454, 1023). But though Stephen has enjoyed a sumptuous education, he has none of their social and economic advantages. On the one hand, there is Buck Mulligan, a witty, urbane, light-hearted but finally unscrupulous and trivial scion of the well-established, well-educated, affluent Catholic middle-classes. Mulligan is shrewdly conscious that he and his own are on their way to power, and relentlessly condescends to Stephen. On the other hand, there is Haines, the Englishman of colonizing stock on whom Mulligan fawns. Stephen himself thinks of Haines as the very figure of 'the seas' ruler' (*U* 9.454, 1023). But he is also, in his own way, a 'constructive Unionist'. 'We feel in England we have treated you rather unfairly', he says. 'It seems that history is to blame' (*U* 1. 648–9).

While fair treatment may be important in cricket, however, it is a concept that can have no meaning in relation to the British

Queen Victoria presides over an anti-Home Rule Bill rally in Belfast, 1912.

presence in Ireland, which was always founded on and sustained by gross historical violence and wrong. Stephen himself broods implacably on historical catastrophe, injustice, dispossession.
He does so all the more pointedly in the second chapter, where he confronts Mr Deasy, the headmaster of the Protestant-dominated school for well-off children at which Stephen is working. Here again, as with Mulligan, the contrast is painfully ironic. Deasy is an Ulster Protestant, and therefore part of a class (the Ulster colons) that, politically, should be playing out its historical and political endgame. But in fact, Deasy is energized by a new sense of who he is and what the prospects of his class are likely to be. For at this point in time, Ulster Unionism was mobilizing quite rapidly. At length, it would demand exclusion from the Home Rule Bill (1912), and eventually partition. In contrast, Stephen is depressed by the Ireland to which he belongs and which, in a sense, he represents. He is dogged by his melancholy awareness that, at this particular

moment, it appears to be going nowhere. In the third chapter, Stephen therefore retreats into what is, in large measure, a theoretical approach to a historical and cultural problem. The trouble with this stratagem is that it leaves him disconnected from life, as Stephen himself uneasily recognizes.

Much of all this was rooted in fact: the School was Clifton School, Dalkey. Buck Mulligan is a fictional equivalent of Joyce's slippery friend Oliver St John Gogarty, with whom Joyce eventually quarrelled, and Haines of Dermot Chenevix Trench. Joyce shared the Martello Tower at Sandycove with the two of them for five days. The crucial difference is that, in reality, this happened in September. Joyce has changed the date, indeed, the time of year. For in the fictional version of 16 June 1904, Stephen's world is entirely dominated by men. He has no Nora. Lacking a Nora, he is without a double boon. For Nora brought Joyce two things. She brought him a love without which, like Stephen's, Joyce's world would very likely have been a rather desolate place. There was nothing ethereal about this love: it flourished off her sexual boldness and, later, her willingness, for example, enthusiastically to participate in the obscene sexual fantasies famously documented in the letters they exchanged in 1909.

Certainly, Joyce was by no means scrupulously faithful to his wife. His brothel life in Trieste, for example, severely tried her patience and loyalty. He became infatuated with students, notably Anna Schleimer and Amalia Popper. But he was also emotionally extremely dependent on Nora. When she went into hospital in Paris, he moved in with her, and Samuel Beckett had to bring him his mail. It was a love that, as friends were later repeatedly to testify, for all the patent differences between their minds and their backgrounds, was quite unusually intimate. They seemed to share a private code. Some of the new friends Joyce later made in Paris rather slighted Nora, or condescended to her. They had a paltry (and quite unJoycean) sense of priorities. When Irish friends like

Arthur Power, Tom McGreevy and Elizabeth Curran claimed that the couple understood each other perfectly, they meant exactly that. Whether or not Nora shared James's book-learning made no difference at all.

But if the intimacy was emotional and sexual, it was also cultural. Scholars have tended either to express surprise at Joyce's choice of Nora, or to justify it on other than intellectual and aesthetic grounds. But these remain the sole options only if we keep up the habit of abstracting Joyce to death. Nora was certainly no intellectual. But her and Joyce's intimacy was very much a question of shared knowledge. For Nora brought him a fund of lore from the west of Ireland of which he knew nothing. This was the second thing she gave him. He found it in her language and heard it in the rhythms of her voice, both of which he loved. In a sense, she completed or, at least, massively enhanced the private Joycean encyclopaedia. Joyce constantly pumped her for detail, personal, local, historical. She became 'his portable Ireland'.[27] Like him, she also had a marvellous memory for music, and the two of them were frequently to be heard casually humming Irish songs together. The funeral wreath she chose for him was harp-shaped.

In *Finnegans Wake*, Joyce refers to the ancient *Eiscir Riada*, the first Irish highway that ran from Dublin to Galway. Take a map of Ireland, and draw a line linking the two cities. You have put a girdle about the country. In effect, this is what Joyce did when he took up with Nora. He clasped Ireland to him. He belted most of his work in similar ways. It was thus that he declared its debt to her. *Ulysses* very obviously begins with a fictional version of himself and ends with what is partly one of Nora. If we take Gretta Conroy to be the central figure at the end of 'The Dead', then so does *Dubliners*. So, in a way, does *Finnegans Wake*. A love of such real and symbolic value required no sanction from the two *imperia*. Exemplary rebel-lovers had been declaring their indifference to church and state by scorning the marriage vows at least since Schiller's *Don Carlos*.

For Joyce to cast himself and Nora in this role was by no means necessarily altogether kind to her. Nonetheless, he was determined not to marry, and when, finally, in July 1931, he did so out of consideration for his heirs, significantly – and he knew it had a symbolic value – he did it in London.

Continental Exile

'And here what will you learn more?' says Stephen Dedalus to himself, of Ireland (*U* 2.404). Having found Nora, it was a question Joyce could ask even more pointedly than Stephen. He told her he 'was fighting a battle with every religious and social force in Ireland for her' (*JJ*, p. 176). Given the relative strength of the two antagonists, however, the logical consequence of that battle was flight. By September, Joyce was urging Nora to leave Ireland with him. On 8 October they took the night boat from Dublin, heading for London, but uncertain as to where exactly they might end up. They left London for Paris the very next day, and Paris for Zurich the day after that, arriving in Trieste on 20 October. Joyce had hoped to teach English at the Berlitz School in Trieste. In fact, he had to start at the Berlitz School in Pola, 150 miles south. After four months, he and Nora returned to Trieste itself. It would be their home for a long time to come.

That Joyce and Nora went precisely where they did was largely a matter of chance. Nonetheless, the speed with which circumstances propelled them deep into Europe, indeed, into what was then known as central Europe, was remarkable. In 1904, 37,413 people left Ireland in hopes of a better future. Most if not all of them were economic migrants. But that was not the self-image that suited Joyce. His 'situation', he told his brother, was one of 'voluntary exile' (*JJ*, p. 194), as befitted an artist and intellectual. There was of course an element of literary self-modelling involved in this. Dante, whose work Joyce loved and could quote in Italian by the page, was certainly part of it. After all, Joyce found himself 'in exile' in the same part of the world as Dante had done six centuries before him. He would have remembered references to some of its towns in the *Divine Comedy*. For example, Pola features in Canto IX of the *Inferno*. Joyce also knew of plenty of other great writers who had gone into exile before him, not least Mediterranean exile. Some of them – Ovid, Shelley, Byron, Wilde – were among his personal favourites. They included writers who, like himself, had declared their own exile, rather than having exile thrust upon them. However, the specific form of European exile that Joyce chose was distinct in two other ways. To understand it fully, we have to go back into Irish history again, this time further than before.

First, by propelling himself into Europe in the way he did, Joyce identified with the tradition of the Irish 'saints and scholars' who had been a civilizing presence in Europe during its dark ages. From the end of the Roman Empire to the rise of Charlemagne and well beyond, the intellectual power of the early Irish Church invigorated an often bleak, barbarian and war-torn continent (including England). The sixth and seventh centuries saw the emergence of the *scoti peregrini*, the Irish wandering saints.[28] St Columcille, St Fursey, St Germanus, St Fiacre, St Frigidian, St Killian, St Gall and, above all, the man Joyce called 'the fiery Columbanus' (*U* 2.144): these are just a few of the Irish missionaries of the period. In the words of scholar Louis Gougaud, they became some of the foremost 'revivers of the intellectual life' of the Europe of the time.[29] They spread learning, built churches and monasteries and founded religious communities. They were renowned for their fervour. When Joyce referred in *Ulysses* to Columbanus' 'holy zeal' (*U* 2.144), whether consciously or not, he was echoing the Venerable Bede. Bede and his contemporaries particularly remarked on the zeal of the Irish saints.

Zeal has become extremely unfashionable. Even the word smells old and musty. But the Irish missionaries were driven by a seemingly limitless passion for their work. Columbanus was famous for a number of Joycean virtues: discipline, unstinting labour, command of language, an eclectic range of knowledge, warmth of heart. Columbanus had the extraordinary 'moral courage' that Joyce's brother Stanislaus saw in Joyce himself,[30] and which fuelled Joyce's tigerish persistence in his task. But, above all, Columbanus' contemporaries associated him with two qualities: enthusiasm (remembering that the word originally means 'possession by a god'), and the *perfervidum ingenium Scotorum*, the lightning genius of the Celts. In *Ulysses*, Buck Mulligan tells Stephen that 'you have the cursed jesuit strain in you, only it's injected the wrong way' (*U* 1.109). We might say the same of Joyce and the zeal of Columbanus.

The saints were followed by the scholars. The most notable of these was the great theologian and philosopher John Scotus Erigena. Erigena had perhaps the finest and most original mind of the early Middle Ages. Among other things, he was remarkable for his knowledge of Greek, unusual in the Latin-centred culture of the time. He became master of the Palatine Academy at the court of King Charles the Bald. He was a man with an adventurous, boldly speculative mind, and his ideas shocked the conservative French intelligentsia. Some reviled his work as an invention of the Devil. Others claimed that he turned established forms of thought into *pultes Scotorum* (Irish porridge). Joyce occasionally confused the life of 'the great heresiarch' with that of the very different figure of Duns Scotus (*CW*, p. 113). But he also described Erigena's work as innovative, 'a life-giving breath working a bodily resurrection of the dead bones of orthodox theology' (*CW*, p. 114). Joyce was well aware of the parallels between Erigena and himself. He keenly identified with 'the Irish nation's desire to create its own civilization'. He even saw himself as its supreme representative. It was not the desire of 'a young nation', however, but of 'an ancient nation' concerned to renew the glories of the past 'in a modern form'. 'The school of apostles' was chief amongst these glories. Erigena had been a spearhead of 'its intellectual force in Europe' (*CW*, pp. 111–14).

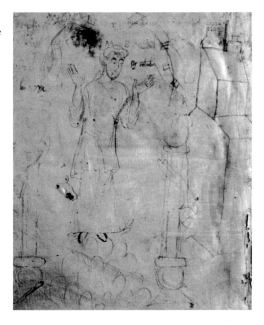

The archetypal, if not the first, exile from Ireland: St Columcille, from a 9th-century MS of Adamnán's *Life of Columba*.

By the nineteenth century, some of the saints and scholars had taken on symbolic importance. Columcille, for example, apparently left Ireland after a quarrel over a copy of a psaltery turned into an actual battle. This gave later generations a pretext for turning him into 'the archetypal if not the first exile from Ireland'.[31] The deracinated and sometimes alienated condition the saints chose was often paradoxically entwined with a fierce devotion to their native land. Exile was an expression, not of estrangement, disenchantment or disloyalty, but of attachment to home and people. So at any rate it seemed, to some who came long after them. 'If I die', said Columbanus, 'it shall be from the excess of the love that I bear the Gael.'[32] The loss of place was inseparable from an intense feeling for it. This was a matter, not just of vague and sentimental nostalgia, but of immersion in particulars. Columcille was a writer who evoked beloved localities from afar. He became the paradigm of the Irishman domiciled abroad, 'thinking longingly in a foreign land of the little places he knew so well'.[33] So, too, in Joyce's case, the condition of what he called exile encouraged an absorbed recollection of a particular locality in all its myriad detail. Thus when he claimed that he wanted *Ulysses* to give so ample and precise a picture of Dublin on 16 June 1904 that the city could be rebuilt from his book, he was not proudly announcing some kind of pre-emptive modernist strike. He was acknowledging how far his work continued and revivified an ancient, Irish Catholic tradition.

The second form of Irish exile that is important for understanding Joyce is political. The significant beginnings of the tradition of political exile lie in the sixteenth century. In the 1530s, the tenth Earl of Kildare, Thomas Fitzgerald, known as Silken Thomas, led a rebellion against Henry VIII. Joyce refers to it repeatedly. The rebellion failed, and the family of the Geraldines were banished. In the 1580s, the Desmonds of Munster also rose. They, too, were duly crushed. But the result on both occasions was that hundreds of defeated Irish rebels went into military service in Europe. This became a tradition, one from which the armies of France, Spain, Austria and Holland all benefited. The defeat of the Irish at the battle of Kinsale in 1601 led to the ensuing 'Flight of the Earls' in 1607. The Cromwellian depredations of 1649–50 and the subsequent settlements of Ireland had similar effects. If, however, in Matthew Arnold's quotation from Ossian that O'Madden Burke 'greyly' recycles in *Ulysses*, the Irish rebels 'went forth to battle . . . but they always fell' (*U* 7.572-73),[34] Ireland's loss was continental Europe's gain. The Irish called their political exiles 'wild geese'. The term was in circulation from 1607. But it was particularly used to describe the men who fled to Europe with Patrick Sarsfield after William of Orange's victory at the Battle of the Boyne and the Treaty of Limerick in 1691. They were followed in their turn, throughout the eighteenth century, by Irishmen intent on serving the Jacobite cause; by members of the United Irishmen in the 1790s; by Young Irelanders after the failure of the 1848 rebellion; and by IRB and Fenian exiles like James Stephens and John O'Leary, notably after the Fenian uprising in 1867.

Even today, wrote Joyce, 'the flight of these Wild Geese continues' (cw, p. 124). He closely identified with the tradition of Gaelic emigration as political exile in Europe. Indeed, importantly, he identified with it at the expense of the alternative tradition – of exile as fresh start in the New World – that had developed from the late eighteenth century. Joyce always resisted the idea of going to America and, until *Finnegans Wake*, at least, showed comparatively little interest in American Irish traditions. In 'Fenianism: The Last Fenian', he paid tribute to John O'Leary, the last of the great political exiles. Even more significantly, in *Ulysses*, he has young Stephen Dedalus pay his visit to Egan in Paris. From at least 1795, when revolutionary Wolfe Tone had ended up there, once Irishmen went into political exile in Europe, other Irishmen started making pilgrimages to them. This is the point to Stephen's encounter with Egan. Joseph Casey turned out to have a fund of stories about classic figures and events from Fenian and IRB mythology. But beyond that, Egan also evokes the bequest of a tradition, though its frail condition effectively marks its political close: 'Weak wasting hand on mine. They have forgotten Kevin Egan, not he them. Remembering thee, O Sion' (*U* 3.263–4). Egan recalls the 'flame of vengeance' of the Fenian bombing of Clerkenwell gaol in 1867 (*U* 3.248). In *Ulysses*, the pacifist Joyce produced what contemporary Shane Leslie described as 'an attempted Clerkenwell explosion in the well-guarded, well-built, classical prison of English literature'.[35]

The wild geese fled to the strongholds of Catholic Europe, from which they could continue to oppose the conqueror, if in less immediate ways than had been the case in Ireland. They looked back almost obsessively to an Ireland to which they knew they were unlikely to return. In both respects, Joyce took after them. Political exile also bred a preoccupation with the figure of the 'leader overseas' or the 'lost leader'. This expressed itself in a number of different forms, particularly poetry, as in the case of the vision-poem or *aisling*. Exiles were memorialized, turned into potential saviours of Ireland, identified with Irish hopes for the future. The redeemer from over the water would free Ireland from its bondage. Joyce certainly thought of his art as having a potentially redemptive function. At times, with varying degrees of irony, he was even inclined to see himself as a Moses-figure. In *Exiles*, the play he wrote in 1914–15, he provided an (admittedly rather idiosyncratic) version of the Irish redeemer.

Richard Rowan is an Irish writer. He bears the name of Archibald Hamilton Rowan, one of the United Irishmen who sought refuge in France (though he explicitly asserts that he is not a descendant). Like Joyce, Richard has spent years in Italy, but has recently returned to Dublin with Bertha, his wife, and his son. Here, Joyce wrote, austerely, Richard must pay the penance his nation exacts from an Irish exile on his return. Richard's friend Robert Hand thinks of him as a Catholic theologian *manqué*, and he has a point. Like Erigena, Richard is a free spirit. He is a radical critic of 'social conventions and morals' (*E*, p. 148). But he also has a streak of Columbanus' intensity and high-mindedness. Where Richard is Catholic, Robert is of Protestant stock, 'a descendant of the dark foreigners', as he says himself, adding that 'that is why I like it here' (*E*, p. 57). He partly patronizes Richard as a man of 'wild blood' (*E*, p. 73). At the same time, he wants Richard to return to Ireland as a cultural hero, to be laden with honours by his people (which, implausibly enough, he seems to equate with becoming a university professor). Richard associates Robert with a will to possess in dispossessing others, and an inability wholly and freely to give. As with Haines in *Ulysses*, the fact that he has a conscience does not make him wholly pardonable.

The play hinges on Robert's pursuit of Bertha. It is clear that, for his own reasons, Richard has connived in this, and even planned it. The penance of the returned exile is prodigality, self-expenditure, an unconditional gift of self. Joyce said that *Exiles* was about the extreme rarity of love understood as goodness, the desire for another's good. Richard wants 'the very immolation of the pleasure of possession on the altar of love' (*E*, p. 149). It is therefore imperative that he assert no mastery, no rights of ownership over his wife. He must allow Bertha complete liberty. Yet, at the same time, in achieving this goodness, he aims at self-liberation. Richard defeats the predator in three ways. First, as he says, by giving in utter freedom, he properly owns what the predator must otherwise threaten to take. Second, the power of the predator is the power to lease one's possessions back to one if he so chooses. Richard refuses to grant Robert this power. Third, the gift freely given cancels any need to take up arms against the predator, or do violence to him. What it most crucial to Richard – as it will later be to Joyce, when, in *Ulysses* and *Finnegans Wake*, he addresses the language, literature and culture of the invader – is to rise superior to both the dispossessor and the fact of dispossession.

At the end of the play, it is not entirely clear whether Robert and Bertha have been lovers or not. But this is not what is most important: as Richard has refused to assert any power over Bertha, so Robert has been unable to assert any power over Richard. In the end, therefore, historical necessity and moral logic together decree that it is now Robert who must go into exile. Appropriately enough, this will be with his aptly named cousin, 'Jack Justice . . . in Surrey. He has a nice country place there and the air is mild' (*E*, p. 136). Joyce's last note on the play refers to 'the adulterous wife of the King of Leinster who brought the first Saxon to the Irish coast' (*E*, p. 160). The allusion is to Devorgilla, who eloped with Dermod MacMurrough. This led to his deposition and flight to England, where he petitioned Henry II for aid, thus helping to provoke the first Anglo-Norman invasion of Ireland. For Joyce, this was not a misogynistic tale. Evil in *Exiles* is not the generous desire to yield to the other, be the desire Irish or female, but the will to exploit that desire, the unscrupulous will to possess (or dispossess) another.

8

Looking Back: *Dubliners*

Exiles partly supplies us with an account of the Joycean logic of exile. But, in a sense, that is true of almost all of Joyce's work before *Ulysses*. Joyce's great collection of short stories, *Dubliners*, is about Dublin at the turn of the twentieth century. In other words, it is about the Dublin Joyce left, and helps to explain why he left it. The death of his mother affected him greatly. He saw her as a victim, not only of his father's improvidence, but of a 'system' that had increasingly condemned her to abject destitution. 'When I looked on the face that I saw in the coffin', he wrote to Nora, in 1904, 'I understood that I was looking at the face of a victim and I cursed the system which made her a victim' (*L* 2, p. 48). The imagery with which Joyce associates Stephen's mother in *Ulysses* – waste, dereliction, decay – is also the imagery he connected with the Dublin of *Dubliners*. 'It is not my fault', he complained, 'that the odour of ashpits and old weeds and offal hangs around my stories' (*JJ*, p. 222). Church and state had left his mother with none of his own will to self-determination, no mental power to combat the circumstances in which she found herself. The same was true of Dublin, too.

Like other modern writers from Baudelaire to Iain Sinclair, Joyce was an inveterate city-prowler. He spent many hours walking in Dublin, not least its 'Nighttown'. Dublin in 1904 was possibly the most impoverished European city outside Russia. According to contemporary reports, in Dublin, unlike other British cities, the 'purlieus' were 'to be met with everywhere';[36] in other words, there

'Houses of decay, mine, his and all' (*U*, 3.105): early 20th-century Dublin slums.

was a slum round every corner. The poor had been increasingly crowding into the city since the Famine. They were not segregated or screened off from other citizens. After the demise of the Irish parliament in 1800, many affluent and powerful Dublin families had left their grand houses untenanted. The poor took them over. Unlike, say, Zola in Paris, Joyce did not write about the urban poor, or directly address their concerns. But he was aware that the economic distinction between the characters in his novels and the classes beneath them was small and precarious. Dublin was a city with imposing traditions, as Joyce ironically underlines in the story 'Two Gallants'. By the early twentieth century, however, it was a city of soiled and faded grandeur and the capital of 'the most belated race in Europe' (*CW*, p. 150). In *Dubliners* – which he referred to as his 'chapter of the moral history of my country' (*JJ*, p. 221) – Joyce set out to tell it as much.

'It is high time', Joyce wrote, 'that Ireland finished once and for all with failures' (*CW*, p. 125). In the first instance, he meant political failures, not personal ones. Again and again, Ireland had failed successfully to resist the conqueror and blaze its own way to independence. This was the case, not least, because, while it fulminated unceasingly against British rule, it remained blithely willing to accept the continuing hold of Rome on its soul. *Dubliners* is a book full of personal failures. In 'The Sisters', a disappointed and apparently disgraced priest dies a melancholy, solitary death. In 'Eveline', a young Irishwoman cannot find the courage or the vitality to keep her promise to elope with her lover. In 'After the Race', an Irishman squanders his patrimony in a drunken night of cards with a group largely composed of more sophisticated Europeans. These rather desolate tales are typical of *Dubliners*. If Joyce's presentation of them is never merely pathetic, that might chiefly seem to be because he stays clinically distant from his material, in the scientific spirit of Zola, or the Flaubert he so admired, and from whom he learnt so much.

But in fact, Joyce repeatedly indicates that, in the Dublin he fled, personal and political failure were everywhere bound up in one another. The first form of failure everywhere reflects, embodies and comments on the second. 'Ivy Day in the Committee Room' places the theme of historical failure in political terms, by emphasizing the stagnation of political hopes after the fall of Parnell and the insignificance of the political figures that followed in his wake. Their broken political will leaves them incapable of continuing his political struggle. 'Grace' places the same theme in relation to the contemporary state of the Irish Catholic church, stressing the spiritual and intellectual inanition of its adherents, the grubby worldliness of the clergy. These two stories serve as large-scale accounts of institutional and cultural forces pervasively at work in Joyce's characters' lives. But as often as not, it is really tiny details that give the game away. In 'A Painful Case', a staid but not uncultivated bank cashier called Duffy frigidly recoils from the woman whose emotional life he has awakened. Her disappointment leads her to drink, and later to her death. Joyce does not condemn Duffy. But, at the same time, he slyly places a copy of the *Dublin Evening Mail* in his pocket. This is rather like giving a copy of the English *Daily Mail* to a present-day English character with intellectual pretensions. Duffy may read Nietzsche and attend meetings of the Irish Socialist Party. But his copy of the *Mail* reveals aspects of him that are more fundamental than either of these activities, both in terms of temperament (unadventurous, conservative) and politics and culture (Unionist).

Joyce was telling stories of the ineluctable failure of the psyche under the conditions of a colonial politics, culture and economy. In 'Counterparts', a clerk gets into trouble at his office, compensates by drinking the evening away, then, smouldering with anger, vengefulness and humiliation, returns home to beat his small boy. The two key moments in his downfall are his confrontation with his Ulster Protestant boss Alleyne, who treats him as a lowly, shiftless Celt, and his comprehensive defeat at the hands of English drinking companion Weathers. Weathers not only appears to possess a nonchalant sophistication and social and sexual ease quite beyond Farrington. He even beats him at arm-wrestling, twice. What matters, in both cases, of course, is not that either Alleyne or Weathers consciously behave like colonizers. It is rather that they behave *enough* like colonizers to trigger a version of a colonial phantasmagoria in Farrington's mind. Similarly, in 'A Little Cloud', Little Chandler feels the smallness of his life exposed and rebuked by his more successful and cosmopolitan friend Gallaher. But what Joyce points out is that subservience is written into all Chandler's ambitions. For they focus, not on Dublin, but on London. The lack of self-assertion which Chandler so bitterly regrets in himself is not merely an unfortunate character trait. It is a product of his culture; or rather, the fact that his culture is not his own, that his imaginative life has been borrowed from elsewhere.

Dubliners is very much concerned with the ways in which colonial Irish society structures relations to which status and power are central. It anatomizes those relations with compelling power and subtlety, and what it shows is bleakly clear. The exploitation and brutalization on which a colonial society is historically founded reproduce themselves at various different levels and in various different features of the social pyramid, in relations between employer and employee, man and woman, husband and wife, parents and children and so on. Differences in economic and social standing are in one sense unusually important. Hence the quite extraordinary fuss that characters keep on making over insignificant and trivial sums of money, of footling questions of rank or class. Yet, at the same time, such differences are also negligible. For true power is always elsewhere from the start. It is precisely because, in a colonial society, the vast majority are always and definitively disempowered that they quarrel so ferociously over meagre scraps of privilege.

Most if not all of the main characters in *Dubliners* bear traces, at least, of Mangan's spiritual affliction, 'vastation of soul' (*cw*, p. 58). Soul, like zeal, is a mildewed word. But *Dubliners* is a chronicle of damaged souls, as perhaps supremely exemplified in the sexual pervert in 'An Encounter', pleading in vain, through a clouded imagination, for some little measure of understanding. The poignancy of the characters in *Dubliners* comes of their closeness to sheer nullity. The damage has been done by the imperial powers. They have offered their subjects forms of thought and feeling that have not provided them with any adequate spiritual sustenance. As Joyce became increasingly aware, however, the crucial problem is not the colonizers' imposition of alien forms on the Irish mind. This is where he differed from those of his contemporaries who wished to see Ireland 'de-Anglicized'. The real trouble is that his Dubliners have not yet taken possession of the colonizers' forms, transformed them, and thereby made them their own. In that respect, they have remained subdued.

Joyce was saying something delicate and complex in *Dubliners*. He was therefore walking an aesthetic tightrope. The possibility of misinterpretation was all too likely. Critics have repeatedly read the volume as expressing a newly European artist's expression of lofty disdain for a provincial and benighted culture. This was certainly not the way Joyce saw it. Even less appetizing characters like 'poor Corley' and 'poor Ignatius Gallaher' deserved compassion. For they were 'fledglings' poised on the edge of modernity, and scarcely grown (L 2, p. 199). 'I have taken the first step', Joyce wrote, 'towards the spiritual liberation in my country' (JJ, p. 221). He was holding up to Dublin the looking-glass that it needed, thereby aiding the cause of modern Irish civilization. This was not a task which separated him off from his people. It was certainly not a task which cast him in the role of superior judge. When, later, Georg Goyert proposed *So Sind Sie in Dublin* (*What They're Like in Dublin*) as the title for the German translation of *Dubliners*, Joyce protested. 'It is not my point of view', he wrote (L 3, p. 164). He preferred *So Sind Wir in Dublin* (*What We're Like in Dublin*).

The social anatomist intent on the liberation of his people has been all too easily confused with that more familiar figure particularly beloved of the Anglo-Saxon tradition, the moral critic concerned to score points. By the time he had completed all bar the last of the stories, Joyce seems to have become aware of the problem himself. He began to fear he had been 'unnecessarily harsh' on Dublin. He had not reproduced any of the attractions of the city. In particular, he had not reproduced 'its ingenuous insularity and its hospitality' (JJ, p. 231). Thus, having finished all the other stories by mid-1906, in 1907, he set out to add another, one much longer and more complex in its implications than the others. It turned into the paragon of modern short stories, 'The Dead'.

'The Dead' (probably) takes place on 6 January, the Feast of the Epiphany. The story does indeed partly bear witness to a generosity and hospitality of which the previous stories had given little sign, notably in the Christmassy atmosphere at the Misses Morkans' annual dance. Here, for the first time, the volume floods with liveliness and warmth. For all Joyce's expressed intentions, however, *Gemütlichkeit* is not what is most important in 'The Dead'. The story is chiefly concerned with Gabriel Conroy and his wife Gretta. Gabriel is the fortunate beneficiary of a 'superior education' that he feels rather raises him above those around him (*D*, p. 203). In particular, though he loves and is happy in his wife, he also patronizes her.

Not surprisingly, he has not always had a very good critical press. But Joyce was less concerned to fasten on his supposed faults than to lay bare an inward predicament and its relation to the state of a culture at a precise historical moment. It is the state of this culture that determines what Gabriel is capable of being, and what not. On the one hand, he and his aunts and their family have acquired a patina of bourgeois respectability. On the other hand, the badges of this respectability repeatedly turn out to be more or less explicitly Unionist, that is, English or English-oriented. For this very reason, however, they are also secondhand. They tend to be faded and threadbare. At one remove, they have lost their gloss. Hence Gabriel's vulnerability, his secret plunges from seeming assurance into insecurity, 'agitation', fear of 'utter failure' (*D*, pp. 179, 204). His culture neither grips nor truly empowers him. It is a shell within which he partly cowers.

Gretta is very different. She, like Nora, hails from Galway. She also has a spiritual life that is not only beyond her husband's experience, but quite beyond his comprehension, too. It is the reef on which Gabriel's fragile self-possession finally runs aground. The denouement of the story hinges precisely on their disparity. At the end of the evening, Gabriel sees a woman whom, for a moment, he does not recognize, listening in rapt attention to the voice of a man singing. It is his wife. This moment inaugurates a process in which, during the rest of the story, Gabriel's assumption of familiarity with his wife progressively dissolves. They return to their hotel, Gabriel full of a mixture of uxorious and lustful emotions that he expresses in the only terms available to him, those of a genteel, rather sentimental, late-Victorian and Edwardian rhetoric. Then Gretta reveals that the song she heard mattered to her as it did because it was sung to her by a delicate lover of her youth. She believes he died for her.

Unresentful, with his wife asleep, Gabriel contemplates the lesson to be learnt from what he takes to be his humiliation. He decides that 'the time had come for him to set out on his journey westward' (*D*, p. 205). It is certainly doubtful whether Gabriel will make this journey, and, even if he does, whether he will be capable of it in anything other than a rather superficial sense. But at this point Joyce takes over, completing Gabriel's initial gesture with a great sweep of haunting, beautiful, intensely melancholic prose evoking the snow-strewn landscapes of the west. The theme, above all, is the connection between the west of Ireland and death. It has several aspects: mythologically, the west of Ireland was the land of the dead. But more significant is the song to which Gretta listens so intently, *The Lass of Aughrim*. The song summons up a history of oppression and grief. On the one hand, the 'lass' is a peasant girl who is refused admission by the lord whose dead child she bears in her arms. She drowns herself. On the other hand, the reference in the name of Aughrim is to defeat, to historical collapse. The battle of Aughrim in 1691 has some claim to having been 'the most disastrous battle of Irish history'.[37] Amidst havoc and brute carnage, William of Orange's army clinched its victory over Catholic Ireland and finally 'broke the back of Gaelic civilization'.[38]

It is thus no coincidence that 'The Dead' includes the image of a horse and cart circling round a statue of 'King Billy'. Just beneath the surface of the ending of the story, however, lies a still starker theme. It was the west, above all, that had suffered from the Famine. In the 1840s, it had been quite literally corpse-littered, to an extent that left foreign visitors mute with awe. For Joyce's generation, the Famine was by no means a historical memory that had comfortably faded into the distance. In any case, there were still outbreaks of famine in the west as late as the 1890s. A thought of the Famine

The village funeral of a victim of the Famine, 1846.

is even instructive for *Dubliners* as a whole: the paralysis and inertia of the culture and people Joyce describes, what I called their closeness to nullity, is post-catastrophic. There is no explicit mention of the Famine in 'The Dead'. But no Irish reader could have responded to its sublime final paragraph without calling the Famine to mind. Of course, while the story gets close to breaking decisively with cosy interiors, it does not do so altogether. Joyce is exquisitely discreet. The sublimity is by no means untouched by irony. Joyce means us to keep Gabriel's warm hotel room and our own equivalents of it firmly in mind. The world of the Famine dead is not Gabriel's, or ours. The ending of 'The Dead' is none the less an epitaph. It is Joyce's oblique homage to a history of suffering, paid in the knowledge that the rest of his work, whilst continuing to bear the burden of it, will also point beyond it.

9

A Second Outpost of Empire

In some important ways if not in others, Joyce, Kafka and Faulkner belong together. All three wrote out of defeated or minority cultures (Irish Catholic, Prague Jewish, American Southern) that were marginal to a massively dominant power (British, Habsburg, Yankee). All three had an uneasy relationship with the dominant culture. For Joyce and Kafka, at least, this was partly a question of language. All three addressed, questioned and transformed a set of dominant cultural and discursive formations. In the process, all three became crucial figures in the movement that we now know as modernism.

But there is one other novelist of the period whose closeness to Joyce was clear to Brecht but has much less often been noted: Jaroslav Hašek.[39] In *Ulysses*, Joyce created the great modern Irish national epic. But, because his epic springs from a historically subjugated culture, it is markedly different to, say, the *Iliad*, the *Aeneid*, *Paradise Lost* or *The Epic of Gilgamesh*, in a way that makes it modern. The same is true of Hašek's modern Czech national epic in prose, *The Good Soldier Schweik*. *The Good Soldier Schweik* everywhere mocks the pomposity, pretentiousness and empty assertiveness of the imperial power and its discourses. Hašek's sensibility was ebulliently demotic, and his stance on the arrant and brutal injustice of the Austro-Hungarian Empire is unsentimentally, toughly comic. Schweik himself is an enormously likeable character, resilient, astute, yet also oddly innocent. The novel is saturated in Czech

Schweik and Austrian authority: a drawing by Josef Lada for Jaroslav Hašek's *The Good Soldier Schweik* (1921–3).

popular culture, everyday Czech life and values. From time to time, Schweik tries to show some feeling for the higher things of life, but elevation is not his style. He is at ease with error and physical grossness. His natural habitat is the inn or bar, and he has an entertainingly scatological wit. In these and other respects, he resembles either the Joyce of *Ulysses*, or Bloom, or both. Joyce himself was by no means as antagonistic towards the Austro-Hungarian Empire as Hašek. After all, it was not the one that really mattered to him. In comparison to the British Empire, it was a ramshackle but by no means repellent affair. He wished, he said, that more empires were like it. Nonetheless, he wrote a skit in doggerel on the Austro-Hungarian monarch that is very like one he wrote on Edward VII.[40] It would have fitted neatly into *Schweik*.

The world of *The Good Soldier Schweik* is ethnically diverse. In that respect, it is historically realistic. It accurately reflects both the ethnic diversity of the Austro-Hungarian Empire and the racial stratifications according to which it operated. Hašek's novel fizzes with hostility towards the Austrians. It is not just evident in Schweik. It shows in a host of Hašek's characters. The Austro-Hungarian Empire became a remarkably fertile breeding-ground for political and cultural dissent. When Joyce moved to Trieste, it was precisely in a corner of this breeding-ground that he found himself. Like Dublin, Trieste was an outpost of Empire, but an important one. After Vienna and Hašek's Prague, it could claim to be the third great Imperial city. To a large extent, it had even been an imperial creation: in the eighteenth century, the Austrians wanted a Mediterranean port. None the less, the Italians had been claiming it as their own since 1848, stirring up a good deal of patriotic Austrian outrage in the process.

Joyce returned to Trieste from Pola in the spring of 1905. This may have been partly because of a significant brush with the imperial Austrian administration. According to Crivelli, at least, after 'an episode of Irredentist espionage', all the foreigners in Pola were ordered to leave,[41] Irredentism being the Italian political movement which, since 1878, had called for the union with Italy of all Italian-speaking districts not under Italian rule. Joyce now found work at the Berlitz in Trieste. He had not liked Pola much. It was a military port, and the pupils he had taught were Austrian naval officials. But Trieste was different. It was rich in colours and styles of life. It buzzed with different voices, accents, tongues. Joyce was very aware of the Austro-Hungarian ethnic and linguistic mix, 'its hundred races and thousand languages' (L 1, p. 57). This mix was abundantly evident in Trieste, and a major cause of its indomitable vitality. Trieste introduced Joyce to Christian churches – Greek and Serbo-Orthodox, for example – quite different to those with which he was most familiar. The city was known as 'the gateway East'. It had been particularly important to Austria as a trading link with the Levant and beyond, and Eastern cultures had left their marks on it.[42] These, too, were an important part of Joyce's Triestine experience.

Yet, in many ways, Trieste was like Dublin. As Crivelli points out, the resemblance was partly physical: the wide bay, the grey neo-classical buildings reminiscent of the Georgian flowering in Ireland, the Canal Grande, all had Dublin equivalents. Trieste, like

Dublin, also had its slums. The extensive old city (and brothel area) was a stinking maze of dark, rubbish-strewn alleys and crumbling hovels above small, dirty, shit-littered canals. Joyce came to know it very well. In rainy weather, black water came squirting out from under the paving stones, just as, famously, it did in the Irish capital, which is why it was known as 'dear, dirty Dublin'. The health problems in the old city were chronic, many of them resembling those common among the poorer classes in early twentieth-century Dublin: chest complaints, especially tuberculosis; circulatory illnesses; congenital disorders; diseases bred by poor sanitation. At the beginning of the century, the mortality rate in Trieste was even higher than that in Dublin, and both were almost the worst in Europe.

The similarities between Trieste and Dublin were also political, as Triestine nationalists were themselves aware.[43] Trieste was a hotbed of Irredentism. However, a very substantial part of the population of Trieste, though Italian-speaking, was actually of Slovene stock, and Slovenes were predominant in the surrounding area. There was also an ample sprinkling of the other peoples of the Empire in Trieste, particularly other Slavic races, but also Jews. The Austrian politics of race was everywhere. The system of racial hierarchy in the Austro-Hungarian Empire was underpinned by racial doctrines that carefully distinguished the 'master' from the 'subject' races. This allowed the Italians, like the Hungarians, while obviously less 'masterful' than Germans, to claim superiority over other races, particularly the Slavic ones. In fact, Trieste enjoyed a cultural pecking-order that was rather like the one that obtained in Dublin. Furthermore, like the British in Ireland, the Austrians operated by divide-and-rule, playing off races and factions against each other as political advantage required. This was as true in Trieste as elsewhere. Not surprisingly, the city bubbled with tensions and resentments, which in turn spelled surveillance, police control. When Joyce lectured in Trieste, his lectures required police authorization, and police observers attended them. 'Passed without incident', said one report.[44]

In effect, Trieste was a city that partly mirrored Joyce's own. But there were also large, key differences. These differences turned out to be crucial to his work. They helped him to think about Dublin from inside and outside. When he left Trieste for a while, in July 1906, to work in a bank in the most ancient and enduring of all imperial capitals, Rome, he hated it. Rome was the seat of the Pope. His 'you-be-damned, Kissmearse' infallibility (*L* 2, p. 189) did nothing to endear the city to Joyce. Even the sound of Rome was unpleasant. Romans were distinguished chiefly by their habit of 'the breaking of wind rereward' (*JJ*, p. 228). When Joyce heard the voices of English tourists echoing round the Colisseum, themselves full of the weight of an imperial history – 'when falls the Colisseum, Rawhm sh'll fall' (*L* 2, p. 168) – the city seemed to bring together the two masters with whom he was most familiar. Trieste was to Dublin as Rome was to London. Not surprisingly, the Roman interlude only lasted until March 1907. Then the Joyces packed and returned to Trieste.

Joyce remained close to Dublin. He stayed in frequent contact with friends and family. He kept up to date with the latest Dublin news. Before very long, he was also busy establishing an Irish family home across the water. His son Giorgio was born in July 1905, his daughter Lucia in 1907. He invited his brother Stanislaus to come and join them in Trieste, where there was now another vacancy at the Berlitz school. Stanislaus arrived in Trieste in October 1905. Stanislaus managed, and repeatedly bankrolled, the Triestine Joyces. He also became more Triestine than James, remaining in Trieste for the rest of his life. Stanislaus later depicted himself as having been the long-suffering victim of a monstrously self-centred, spendthrift, reprobate genius. James's fecklessness certainly severely tested both Stanislaus's practical resources and his patience. But Stanislaus believed in his brother, his mission and his gifts. He even named his son James. His prudence finally stood him in good stead. He survived his ordeal and prospered, marrying into the upper reaches of Triestine society and becoming an established University teacher and well-respected citizen. It was James who originally made this possible. He wanted to 'rescue' at least some family members from the sinking ship of his father's fortunes. Once they arrived, however, they could be made to serve as useful props to a shaky ménage. This also happened with the 'cattolicissime', his 'hyper-Catholic' sisters, Eva and Eileen, whom Joyce brought to Trieste himself. Eva soon fled back to Dublin. Eileen stayed, eventually marrying one of Hašek's fellow-nationals.

If Trieste was like home, it also expanded Joyce in significant and creative ways. Here he became friendly with a range of interesting, educated and often cosmopolitan Jews. As McCourt says, it was only in Trieste that Joyce became intimate with a Jewish community in all its political and cultural complexity.[45] This would of course be very important for his future masterpiece. Culturally, too, Trieste had a lot to offer. It was a city, after all, where Mahler could be heard conducting Wagner. Joyce paid attention to the Italian Futurist movement, which was particularly strong in Trieste, and its passion for new technology. He befriended and promoted the great Triestine novelist Ettore Schmitz, better known as Italo Svevo, a Jew of Swabian origin. Joyce not only enthusiastically absorbed the modern European culture he found in the city. He also tried to export it back to Ireland. He knew that Ireland needed it, too. In 1904, neither Trieste nor Dublin had a cinema. By 1909, however, Trieste had a number, Dublin still none. Trieste was keeping up with the modern world. Dublin was not. Joyce set out to rectify matters. He inspired a group of Triestine businessmen with the idea of setting up cinemas in Dublin, Belfast and Cork, and spent time in Dublin establishing the first one. All too soon, his partners abandoned the project. The modernization of Dublin would have to wait.

Like Gibraltar, which is so important in the last chapter of *Ulysses*, Trieste was a Mediterranean territory ruled by an alien

power. Yet it had managed to survive this domination with no
blatantly traumatic consequences for its culture. It was obstinately
lively and undepressed. For Joyce, this was instructive. Trieste
detached him from Dublin without making him indifferent to it.
It placed Dublin in perspective. In some ways, Joyce inhabited a
middle ground between the two cities, not least politically. He had
a range of different contacts with Irredentist circles and activities.
He knew how much they had in common with Irish nationalists,
not least their constant demand for their own university. Yet,
whilst Stanislaus had serious Irredentist sympathies, James was
wary of identifying too much with the Irredentist cause. Like the
Anglo-Irish nationalists in Dublin, the Irredentists spoke from a
relatively privileged class position. They remained at a distance
from the Slovene majority surrounding them. But Joyce identified
Celts and Slavs, arguing that, 'in many respects', they were very like
each other (*cw*, p. 124). In any case, from 1904 to 1907, he was still
calling himself a socialist. He mixed with socialists both at the
Berlitz School and as a result of his work there. He listened to their
denunciations of the Austrian state and the Catholic Church and
their expressions of distrust for Irredentism. He read some of what
they were reading: Gorky's novels, for instance. He came under
the influence of Italian socialist intellectuals, notably Guglielmo
Ferrero. By 1907, however, he was finding himself increasingly
drawn to the emergent Sinn Féin, and its leader Griffith, whom
he saw as a sensible, pragmatic man.

Joyce's mature politics might be thought of as a variant on Sinn
Féin nationalism, but so far complicated as frequently to seem like
a different politics. There were points at which he closely identified
with the new nationalism, but also major points at which he radically dissented from it; hence his claim to be a 'detached observer'
rather than a 'convinced nationalist' (*cw*, p. 116). Certainly, the
development of Joyce's political thought is clear from the lectures
he gave at the Università Popolare and the articles he wrote for the

nationalist newspaper *Il Piccolo della Sera* between 1907 and 1912. As Kevin Barry has argued, much in both the lectures and the journalism derives from Griffith.[46] Yet, at the same time, the Triestine writings exhibit a complexity of attitude to Ireland, its relation to Britain and the Church that clearly owes a great deal to Joyce's perspective from abroad. Dwelling in complication now became a crucial Joycean principle, and Joyce never abandoned it thereafter. It served as the very foundation of what later became known as his modernism. There are no knee-jerk responses in the Triestine writings. They are essentially thoughtful. Moreover, they are thoughtful in a way that tells us a great deal about the novel that Joyce was working on at the same time, *A Portrait of the Artist as a Young Man*, and the book he would then go on to write, *Ulysses*.

One reason for Joyce's growing commitment to complexity was the lack of any sense of it in English journalism. English journalists were 'disposing of the most complicated questions of colonial polities' with dismaying swiftness and ease.[47] As Barry, again, has shown, Joyce himself set out to reverse the process. This was partly because of his new experiences: in Trieste, he repeatedly came up against a set of stereotypes of and prejudices about the Irish. It was probably almost the first time he had come across them other than from Anglo-Saxons. He became aware – or more vividly aware – that the source of the images of the Irish in circulation in the world at large was English not Irish. His work as a whole between 1907 and 1922 was to some extent powered by an intense desire to rectify this state of affairs. The world had to be told that the Irish were not 'the unbalanced and incapable cretins we read about in the leading articles in the *Standard* or the *Morning Post*' (*cw*, p. 123). Trieste was a very good place to begin to do the telling. For if it exposed Joyce to a measure of casual denigration of the Irish, because of its own political circumstances, it also supplied him with a like-minded public. His lecture audience had Irredentist sympathies. His editor at *Il Piccolo della Sera*, Robert Prezioso, specifically asked him to strike 'not only at the British empire that ruled Ireland but also at the Austrian Empire that ruled Trieste'.[48] In addressing Trieste, Joyce was addressing Ireland, and vice versa.

The new complexity to Joyce's thought about Irish politics and culture comes across most clearly in the first of the three Triestine lectures. It steers a very narrow course between a number of different intellectual positions that have their separate attractions but are finally unpalatable as wholes. This course is so tightly hemmed in that the lecture is repeatedly on the point of self-contradiction. Joyce is partly concerned, as his title suggests, with the Irish conception of 'Ireland, Island of Saints and Sages'. Since he tells his audience that the historical side of this account ought to be treated with a pinch of salt and says that Irish self-assertion should not be based on an appeal to past glories, we might expect this conception to get a hard time. In fact, Joyce dwells almost lovingly on the details of the lives of the holy men, and takes evident pride in their careers in Europe. But these two apparently inconsistent attitudes are bound together by a single logic. Joyce actually makes a double claim for Irish strength. He brings some of the neglected riches of Ireland's cultural history to light. But in urging the need for a discerning and even sceptical view of Irish tradition, he seems shrewd, dispassionate, coolly scientific. In effect, he places himself as representing a new, modern Ireland that can hope to enter the family of modern European nations. Since his claim to modernity is inseparable from a repudiation of mythological forms of knowledge, he also pits himself against the revivalists, who were making a similar claim.

The two-handed logic persists in Joyce's treatment of other themes. Take race: on the one hand, the lecture rightly argues that the Irish are a chronically impure race. Irishness 'is an immense woven fabric in which very different elements are mixed' (*cw*, p. 118). Yet, by the end of the very paragraph in which this argument appears, Joyce is writing of 'the present race in Ireland' and describing it as belonging to the Celtic family. He equates Irish and Celts throughout the essay, and discusses the Irish problem as part of the larger predicament of British Celts. He even goes so far as to assert that, whilst the Irish may be a composite people, it is this in itself that constitutes them as 'a new Celtic race' (*cw*, p. 114). If Irish blood is always mixed, why say, as Joyce does, that most of the heroes of the modern Irish movement had no Irish blood in them? Once again, he is walking a precarious tightrope. He wants to insist on the distinctiveness of Ireland and the significance of its history. But he also wants to set them at a distance, to put both in proportion. For he knows how unmodern this insistence is.

But if the lecture teeters on the edge of paradox, it does so for very good reason. The twilight of colonial rule leaves the writer in a practically impossible situation. He must promote the cause of his own and his nation's future independence. The difficulty lies in knowing how best to think about the national history. It draws the writer into identification, as a history of oppression and suffering that demands respect. It also repels him, because it is a history of failure and subservience. As a history of dependence, it must be surmounted, left behind; yet a conception of freedom that pays no serious and lasting tribute to those who worked, struggled, suffered and died en route to it is a dangerously trivial one. The writer, then, must simultaneously claim and disown the past. He must identify with historical passions and urgencies and remain faithful to historical tragedy, not least because from them derives the struggle for independence itself. Yet he must also point beyond them, because he knows that healthy independence means separation from history, and even a degree of historical oblivion.

Thus 'Ireland, Island of Saints and Sages' says two quite different things about English rule and the English-Irish relation. At one point, Joyce refers to a man tied to a carriage and having his insides whipped out by British troops. In the lecture, at least, this comes quite close to being Joyce's symbol for the English treatment of the

Irish. The English in Ireland have been wantonly brutal, cunning and venal oppressors. Joyce says that repeatedly, and quite baldly. His closeness to Fenian and nationalist tradition made him altogether aware, both of how ruthless an invader England could be, and how unusually good it was at concealing the fact, even from itself. But on the other hand, he is extremely tough-minded. He refuses to opt for Fenian and nationalist outrage. There are no stirring or heart-rending denunciations of the vile injustice of the colonizer. Joyce the modern intellectual and writer defies colonial history by rising superior to it and shrugging it off, whilst everywhere showing that a massive effort is required to do so. It is naïve to rail against the ferocity of a colonial power, he asserts, since ferocity is the name of the colonial game. Indeed, putting up a moral protest even colludes with the colonizer's myth of himself, the idea that there are moral principles at stake in colonial activity. There can be no debate about the morality of Empire. Empires, by definition, are monstrous and unprincipled. This is as true of the Roman Catholic as it is of the British one. The Irish, however, are unhelpfully ambivalent about imperial rule. They fulminate against the English. But 'the tyranny of Rome still holds the dwelling place of the soul' (*cw*, p. 125), and peremptorily throttles any true will to liberty.

The conduct of the colonial overlord, then, is not what matters most. What matters is the possible 'resurgence' of Ireland as a self-assertively modern nation (*cw*, p. 125). The self-assertion in question is spiritual, economic, cultural, material and practical together. Certainly, it means vigorously resisting the two imperial powers at once. But it also means resisting the intimate dependence on or complicity with the enemy that can easily become inseparable from resistance to him. All of Joyce's Triestine writings follow a similarly winding line of thought. Trieste itself helped make him think like that. There is a wonderfully comic scene in *Ulysses* in which the Jewish outsider Leopold Bloom innocently meditates on the arcane mysteries of the Catholic Church, like the Mass:

Nice discreet place to be next some girl. Who is my neighbour?
Jammed by the hour to slow music . . . Now I bet it makes them
feel happy. Lollipop. It does. Yes, bread of angels it's called.
There's a big idea behind it, kind of Kingdom of God is within
you feel. First communicants. Hokypoky penny a lump.
[*U* 5.340–42, 359–62]

Joyce could not have written anything so exhilaratingly blasphemous
without Trieste. Trieste gave him the opportunity to see Ireland
in reverse. The reversed perspective fed his lectures and journalism,
too.

The opportunity lasted until the onset of the First World War.
Then life rapidly became more difficult for the city's foreigners.
In January 1915, the pro-Irrendentist Stanislaus was arrested and
interned in Austria. When, in May 1915, Italy entered the war, on
the opposite side to Austria, of course, the writing was truly on the
wall. Joyce and his family left Trieste in June. When they returned,
in 1919, Trieste was much more like Pola than it had been in 1905.
It was now the Trieste of Victor Emmanuel, a port on the eastern
border of Italy, and rapidly assuming a more sober and provincial
air. Triestine culture had been a lot more vital under imperial
Austria than it was now. Indeed, a free Trieste was by no means
altogether unlike Dublin as it was soon to be, under the new Free
State. Joyce had little taste for the new Trieste, and left for good in
the summer of 1920.

10

The Battle of the Book

There is another story to be told of Joyce's Trieste years. It is the
story of his struggle to get *Dubliners* published. It runs more or
less from the beginning to the end of the Trieste period, and provides
a very important context for understanding Joyce's subsequent
development.

Joyce began work on *Dubliners* in 1904. By the end of that year,
the *Irish Homestead* had published three of the stories. By October
1905, Joyce had completed eleven of them. He sent these stories
to Grant Richards. Richards had started his own publishing firm
in Dublin in 1897, and had made his reputation by publishing
the early work of authors who later became well known. Joyce
seemed likely to interest him, though the fact that the manuscript
of *Chamber Music* (Joyce's collection of poems) had ended up
packed away with some of Richards's furniture might have given
the author a few qualms. For a while, however, all went well.
Richards's reader liked the book. So did Richards himself. He
offered Joyce a contract, which Joyce duly signed.

The trouble began when, in February 1906, Joyce sent Richards
a copy of the story 'Two Gallants'. Richards sent it on to the
printer without reading it. Under English law, both the publisher
and the printer of any indecent or blasphemous material could
be prosecuted. Richards's printer immediately sent 'Two
Gallants' back to Richards with the message 'We cannot print
this'.[49] He seemed to have objected to Joyce's (actually very discreet)

handling of the story's sexual theme. He had similar objections to details in 'Counterparts' (like the mention of a woman brushing against Farrington's chair). Joyce retorted that such details were commonplace even in reports of divorce cases in the *Standard*. The printer must have 'priestly blood' in him (*JJ*, p. 200). For his part, Richards should stop being finicky and help to start changing English literature, which had become 'the laughing-stock of Europe' (*JJ*, p. 220).

Richards, however, was not about to be enlisted in the service of Joyce's struggle against Church and state. Instead, he asked Joyce to omit the word 'bloody' from 'Grace'. Joyce replied that the word appeared elsewhere in the stories, and pleaded the cause he had promoted with Richards from the start, the realism of *Dubliners*. If one of his characters said he was going to bloody well put the teeth of another character down his throat, how could the author alter that, without looking as though he were sanitizing the truth? His work of moral history and spiritual liberation depended upon exactitude. If Richards prevented the Irish people from taking a good look at themselves in Joyce's looking-glass, he would 'retard the course of civilization in Ireland' (*JJ*, p, 222). This, however, was a risk that Richards was willing to take. He agreed to include 'Two Gallants', but only if Joyce would make other changes. Joyce rewrote 'The Sisters' and excised six 'bloodys'. Fearful of bankruptcy, Richards decided this was not a sufficient compromise. In September 1906, he withdrew the offer of publication, and sent the manuscript back to Joyce.

Joyce made some changes to the stories, added 'The Dead', and sent them off to other publishers, in London as well as Dublin, without success. Then, in 1909, he tried Maunsel and Co., a new publishing house in Dublin with close ties with the Anglo-Irish revivalists. Joseph Hone and Ulsterman George Roberts had set it up in the summer of 1905. Roberts was a mystic, sometime

Nietzschean and former seller of women's underwear. He became managing director. He knew Joyce already: he had lent him money before his departure from Dublin, and helped him home when he was drunk. He read *Dubliners*, liked it, and offered Joyce a contract. He even asked George Bernard Shaw to help promote it, and advanced Joyce money on the royalties. Then he began to develop Richards-like anxieties. He, too, worried about some of the characters' language. But he chiefly fastened on a passage in 'Ivy Day' in which one of the characters refers (quite indulgently) to Edward VII as 'an ordinary knockabout' who likes his 'glass of grog' and is 'a bit of a rake' (*D*, p. 148). He asked Joyce to change the passage. Joyce's cursory effort to do so did not satisfy him. Roberts made more demands. Joyce did not respond.

Some might have shrugged off Roberts's misgivings as feeble and squeamish. But Joyce saw him as a loyalist grovelling abjectly before the English monarch. There may have been a point to his doing so: according to Hone, at least, Roberts gave in to the strictures of the Vigilance Committee (whose policy on indecent writings was search-and-destroy) and the moral authority of the Lord Lieutenant of Ireland's wife. Richards's capitulation to Victorian and Edwardian prissiness in matters artistic had been similarly craven. In Roberts's case, however, Joyce rather startlingly decided that the only thing for it was to go to the top. The way to show Roberts how pusillanimous he was being was to get the present king himself, George V, to declare the passage in question to be unobjectionable. George V having proved to be unhelpful – his secretary replied, somewhat grandly, that 'it is inconsistent with rule for His Majesty to express his opinion in such cases' (*JJ*, p. 315) – Joyce turned to the Irish newspapers. He had the passage printed and sent to them, with a covering letter explaining how badly Richards and Roberts had treated him. He made a point of indicting, not just individuals, but a 'system' (*JJ*, p. 315), as he had done with his mother's death. Revealingly and significantly, the only paper to print his submission as a whole was *Sinn Féin*. Whilst neither 'Ivy Day' nor *Dubliners* as a whole could in the least be described as a straightforward expression of familiar nationalist sentiment, it was only *Sinn Féin* that really understood the culture out of which Joyce wrote.

Roberts was not finished yet. He demanded more changes, even larger ones. Joyce, in despair, agreed. But Roberts also wanted financial indemnification against possible prosecution. Joyce, of course, could not supply it. Roberts refused to publish. Joyce offered to omit 'An Encounter', as Roberts had asked, but under certain conditions. Roberts applied to London for judgement (London being the home of his solicitor). The solicitor insisted on financial sureties. Roberts demanded even more changes. Joyce refused to make them. He even turned to Arthur Griffith, since Griffith had published his letter, but Griffith could only sympathize. He knew full well what Roberts was like. Finally, Roberts offered to let Joyce buy back the proofsheets. By a curious irony, the process with Richards was finally reversed, in that, once again, the printer chipped in, but, this time at the end, asserting that he wouldn't publish the unpatriotic material anyway. Joyce could only retire in defeat.

Roberts recognized the strength of Joyce's will. He also understood its roots. 'The Giant's Causeway', he said, 'is soft putty compared with you' (*JJ*, p. 324). His estimation of the balance of power in their relationship may have been disingenuous. It was certainly hardly correct. All the same, the Ulsterman's image speaks volumes. He and Joyce may have glossed their struggle in certain ways for others' benefit, or indeed for their own. It nonetheless bore striking resemblances to the relationship between Alleyne and Farrington in 'Counterparts' and the relationship between Stephen Dedalus and Deasy that Joyce would later evoke in *Ulysses*. The flinty intransigence of a Dublin Catholic rebel intellectual and writer collided with the granite determination of a commercially aware and politically circumspect Belfast Protestant publisher. What is notable is how far Roberts prevailed. In demanding concessions from Joyce to which the author had progressively to agree, he humiliated him as practically no one else had been able to do before or would be able to do afterwards. Though Deasy in *Ulysses* is an old man, Joyce gives him a brisk and robust assertiveness that, for all his manifest intellectual superiority, Stephen lacks, and which even vaguely cows and intimidates the young man. The Roberts story helps to tell us why.

However, Roberts also steeled Joyce in his purposes. In the end, in 1914, Richards published *Dubliners* after all. Nonetheless, after a wearying decade of extremely hard work, Joyce was beginning to see that he needed to turn in a different direction. He also needed some good allies. In a foretaste of things to come, it was a vastly energetic American who came to his aid. In December 1913, he was contacted by Ezra Pound. This marked a turning point in his life and career. Pound was already becoming the extraordinary catalyst, champion of modern art and generous supporter of new writing that would make him so important and influential in the second and third decades of the century. Yeats had mentioned Joyce's name. He, Pound, would be interested in reading, and possibly publishing, some of Joyce's work. Joyce sent him *Dubliners* and the first chapter of *A Portrait of the Artist as a Young Man*. Pound knew great writing when he saw it. He saw that what he read was as good as James or Conrad. From this moment, Joyce was launched, as Richards and Roberts could never have launched him. His approaches to established publishers in London and Dublin had either met with rejection, or been fraught with problems. With Richards and Roberts, at least, the issues might have seemed aesthetic, legal and commercial, but, in fact, were often acutely political. Pound's slogan, by contrast, was 'Make It New!' In practical if not aesthetic, intellectual, cultural and political terms, he offered Joyce a chance to cut straight through the twisted historical knots that had caused him so much trouble. Joyce could continue to write the moral history of his country and to serve the cause of its liberation. But there was no point hoping to do so through its institutions, or those of the conquering power. Henceforth, he would pursue his project under other auspices. The world would learn to call it modernism.

11

Ireland Made Me:
A Portrait of the Artist

The Trieste years were also the years in which Joyce wrote the autobiographical novel which at length became *A Portrait of the Artist
as a Young Man*. 'Many of the frigidities of *The Boarding-House* [sic]
and *Counterparts*', he noted, 'were written while the sweat streamed
down my face on to the handkerchief which protected my collar'
(*SL*, p. 69). The same was presumably true of *A Portrait*. It is an
extraordinary thought, and we might pause on it. The quotation
vividly encapsulates Joyce's acute sense of the difference between
the two environments. It also expresses, not just the difference
between his inner and outer worlds at this time, but their paradoxical
interdependence. In more ways than one, the experience of Trieste
helped him to be exact about what he took to be the chilly desolation
of Dublin.

Joyce had begun an autobiographical novel as early as 1904,
before he left Ireland. The imperative of looking back over his formative years was clearly compelling. The significant early version was
called *Stephen Hero*, though Joyce also produced an essay called
'A Portrait of the Artist'. *Stephen Hero* grew to enormous size. Joyce
began rewriting it as *A Portrait* in late 1907, completing a first revised
chapter by 29 November. Even this he saw as artless and retrograde.
He feared he was resorting to an old bag of tricks that modern
Europe made look obsolete. He went back to work. By 7 April 1908,
he had completed three chapters. Then he stopped, no doubt with
Dubliners in mind, explaining that he feared the English would

prosecute him for pornography. In 1911, still quarrelling with Roberts, in a moment of rage, despair and family-oriented histrionics, he even threw the uncompleted work into the fire, but Eileen fished it out. Joyce rewarded her with three bars of soap and a new pair of mittens. It was only after Pound got in touch that he felt encouraged to finish the book. Pound arranged for it to be published in instalments, in a new and unusual London review, the *Egoist*, of which he was effectively literary editor. Joyce seems to have finished the book at more or less exactly the time he left Trieste.

What should we make of this history of composition? Joyce might conceivably not have finished *A Portrait* at all. There was nothing foreordained about his progress to canonization as a supreme modern genius. He was by no means sure that he was ever going to find a publisher for his work. Throughout the Trieste years, whilst convinced of his gifts, he was often haunted by a fear of possible failure, and made various plans for the future which might very well have meant giving up writing altogether. Yet, at the same time, telling the story of his own life obviously very much mattered to him, enough for him to persevere. This particular drive had nothing to do with egoism or self-display. He needed to understand the circumstances that had made him what he was. For understanding them also involved a recognition of how they might have been different, how similar circumstances might be countered or changed. This recognition meant grasping the specific character of the historical forces that had been formative for him. In other words, it meant grasping their historicity. Joyce had a preternaturally acute sense of historicity. People and cultures obsessively construct patterns to persuade themselves of the enduring sameness of things. Irish colonial society made Joyce quite remarkably disinclined to believe that such patterns had any binding force. His sense of historicity is part of what made him one of the great modern experimenters. It also enabled him, in *Ulysses*, to write the most historically precise novel that has ever been written.

The strange, often bleakly evocative novel that is *A Portrait* took shape on the shores of the Mediterranean. A sense of detachment is intrinsic to it. This is sometimes mistaken for the detachment of the social critic or moralist. In fact, it is more like the detachment of the vivisectionist, a term which Joyce used to proclaim the scientific modernity of his work. He chose the word with particular care. Like the anatomist, the vivisectionist is skilled in cutting up bodies. He or she is an expert on the structure of the body, its parts and their functions. But, unlike anatomy, vivisection is carried out on a living organism, an organism, in principle, still capable of growth. In *A Portrait*, Joyce became the vivisectionist of his own soul.

A Portrait is a late example of the nineteenth-century tradition of the European *Bildungsroman*, the novel concerned with the development and formation of a young man. Exceptionally, however, the young man in question grows up in a culture that is both European and colonial. Three kinds of personal development are at stake in *A Portrait*: first, *Bildung* itself, the 'official' formation of a young man in a particular stratum of colonial society. Joyce shows us very clearly how far the two imperial masters are responsible for this formation. *Bildung* takes place in specific institutions, family, school, university, church. It is also a product of cultural institutions, literature, music and so on. For Joyce, of course, *Bildung* is crucially a question of language, discourse, habits of thought that are verbal habits, too. Second, there is the opposite of *Bildung*, what Thomas Mann wryly called *Entbildung*, the coming apart or dismantling of formations. Mann himself took an almost lascivious delight in watching the German bourgeois psyche crumble, as in the case of Aschenbach in Venice. Joyce's strategy was different.

For Joyce, a novelist of a colonial society little more than a decade from independence, *Entbildung* also implies counter-formation. Counter-formation comes about as a result of counter-discourses (rebellious, anti-colonial, anti-clerical etc.). *A Portrait* handles the relationship between *Bildung*, *Entbildung* and counter-formation with immense subtlety and an extraordinary awareness of hidden ironies. Here we see the Joyce of the Triestine writings as a novelist, picking a precise and delicate path through issues that have become extremely complex for him. In particular, he is painfully but pitilessly conscious of how far counter-formations can seem to oppose established ones whilst actually turning out to consolidate them. The irony at the expense of his hero, the young Stephen Dedalus, is often correspondingly exacting.

But there is also another and much more obscure development at work in *A Portrait*, the sentimental education of the hero. The great European *Bildungsromanen* – Stendhal's *The Red and the Black*, Lermontov's *A Hero of Our Time*, Turgenev's *Fathers and Sons*, Constant's *Adolphe* – all finally indicate the crucial importance of emotional growth, even if only negatively, obliquely or in reverse, in the death or failure of the hero. The process of *Bildung*, and the young man's preoccupation with it, tend to prevent him from recognizing his emotional needs. The results are frequently disastrous. Significantly, Stephen in *A Portrait* does not meet with disaster, because, in the case of the young colonial subject, if not exactly a sham affair, *Bildung* is always precarious. However unwittingly, Stephen tends to hold himself at a certain distance from the process of his own formation, is alienated from it. The process of *Bildung* engulfs him less than it does Bazarov or Adolphe. Nonetheless, Joyce makes it abundantly clear that, at the end of the novel, Stephen still has a great deal to learn.

Stephen's surname is Dedalus. Dedalus was the mythical Greek inventor, sculptor and architect famous for constructing the labyrinth at Knossos to house the Minotaur, but who was then imprisoned in his own construction. From *A Portrait* onwards, Joyce started creating literary labyrinths. His engagements with the Irish historical, political and cultural issues dominating his work are characterized by an increasingly labyrinthine complexity. His art is powered by a profound, intense and historically motivated concern with the assertion of independence. In *A Portrait*, Stephen is characterized by his declarations of independence. However, the determination not to serve finds itself repeatedly caught in the snares of complicity, entanglement, interinvolvement, reversibility.

Joyce's project was, massively, libertarian. But he was also everywhere conscious of the immensely problematic character of any definitive conception of Irish freedom. On this point, he very clearly distinguishes himself from all his Irish republican and nationalist contemporaries. Hence the importance of the figure of the labyrinth, a figure for a kind of complication that may or may not be soluble. In a labyrinth, the victim loses him- or herself in a seemingly endless wilderness of fissures, splits, rifts, divisions. The wilderness threatens to become dispiriting, to sap morale. To seek a path through a labyrinth is repeatedly to choose what may seem to be the better option, only to have it more or less circuitously lead back to the point from which one started. It is to negotiate an intricate way between what will almost invariably turn out to be inadequate alternatives. Paths lead not only to impasse,but back to other paths that one already knows go nowhere. In other words, the labyrinth is a pervasively ironical structure. It is an allegorical figure for Joyce's work from *A Portrait* onwards. It is also a political figure. *A Portrait* is a labyrinthine account of the making of the maker of labyrinths, though, in comparison with the later ones, this labyrinth is admittedly simple.

Stephen's early development is much influenced by the recent successes of Parnellism. In the 1880s, which is when Chapter 1 is set, Parnell was striving to unify Ireland against the dominant power and endow it with unprecedented advantages. The result was conspicuous gains in social status and economic prospects for the Irish Catholic middle class. The Dedalus family in the first chapter of *A Portrait* is buoyed up by the new confidence inspired by Parnell, and Joyce discreetly alludes to the little domestic items that are tokens of a modest new affluence or proper middle-classness.

The trouble is that the family is also partly dancing to another tune within Parnellite culture, that of a concept of gentility and respectability whose model is Victorian English. This is evident enough in Stephen's education at Clongowes. Joyce submits Clongowes to a critique that resembles contemporary nationalist critiques of the colonial education system in Ireland.[50] He also goes beyond them, however, particularly in underlining the connivance of the Church.

Then Parnell falls from grace. The new unity in Ireland starts to break up. In the Christmas dinner scene, what separates Simon Dedalus and Mr Casey from their opponent Dante Riordan is the long, drear shadow of the Church. There are two Joycean lessons to be learnt from this. First, resistance to the state must also be accompanied by resistance to ecclesiastical and priestly authority. Self-assertion and proud independence will depend on a repudiation of the two imperial masters, together. Second, it is important to persist with a Parnellite principle of discipline, deliberation and self-control. Thus, at the end of the chapter, Stephen bravely protests the cause of justice to the Clongowes rector. In miniature, he affirms the value of continuing with Parnell's obduracy and thoughtfulness, combined with the passionate intransigence of Fenianism. Yet Stephen's triumph is also ambivalent, in that his actual expression of the need for justice remains precisely determined by norms whose provenance is Victorian English and genteel.

Chapter 2 covers the years from 1892 to 1898, and charts the slow and welcome corruption of the strain of Victorian respectability in Stephen. After the death of Parnell, the Dedalus family attempts to return to respectable, middle-class life. But the political and economic structures that had made that life feasible are now disintegrating. Respectability becomes an imposture. Joyce slyly charts the widening gulf between pretension and stark economic reality. Stephen responds to his new situation by cultivating the young Joyce's attitude of intellectual detachment and disdain. Like the young Joyce, in doing so, he mimics Parnell. But he is also at the mercy of Parnellite melancholia. He is stalked, almost possessed, by Parnell's ghost.

Stephen becomes aware of his sexuality. Like his Parnellism, this pits him against Church and state, specifically, against Victorian English genteel ideology and Catholic morality. The chapter ends with what appears to be another victory over repressive forces, as Stephen visits a prostitute. But in fact, Stephen's expressions of his sexuality are pervasively marked by the Anglo-Irish revivalism of the 1890s, by Yeats, AE, others too. Stephen articulates his sense of himself through a revivalist stock-in-trade: tropes, syntax, vocabulary, repertoire of scenes, tones, moods and even themes. Above all, he shares the revivalist conviction of historical futility that I remarked on earlier and that is pervasive in revivalist writing at precisely this time. Stephen is trying to express a set of intense and urgent personal emotions. Not surprisingly, he turns to the best Irish writing then current for help. In a sense, there is nowhere else to go. But, in this respect, he remains entrammelled by the dominant culture, even as his sexual interests goad him to subvert it. Indeed, since Parnellite melancholia was very much a feature of '90s revivalism, revivalism even provides the terms for Stephen's self-assertion. Here, again, his proud aloofness turns out to be a form of dependence.

Of course, the gulf between Stephen and the revivalists is evident enough. This is particularly the case with sex and class. The revivalists had little or no overt interest in sex, so Stephen is partly seeking to bend their repertoire to accommodate thoughts and feelings that are foreign to it. Equally, in its most significant forms, the revivalism of the '90s was very much the preserve of a privileged class and thrived off its English connection. We are left painfully aware of how distant Stephen is from the social world implied by much revivalist language. All the same, neither Stephen's proud aloofness nor his sexuality breaks a clear track through the labyrinth. They are rather subjected to the logic of the labyrinth itself, according to which any apparently decisive advance is likely to mean being re-enfolded in the maze. The same logic governs Chapter 3. This chapter is centrally concerned with the Irish Catholic Church as an instrument of *Bildung*. Indeed, so closely is it concerned with the specifics of late-nineteenth-century Irish Catholicism that, according to Svevo, Joyce doubted whether he was going to find a reader who could derive any enjoyment from it.[51] In Chapter 3, the link between revivalist language and Stephen's sexual and emotional life that Chapter 2 established breaks down. Stephen begins the chapter in the same grandiose, vague, Revival-derived mood of 'weariness' that dominated much of Chapter 2. But there are clearly limits to what he can get from the language of revivalism. Hence the temptation to return to the Church, which Joyce slyly charts.

Catholic theology and doctrine provide certain comforts. These comforts are by no means trivial. Catholicism offers an elaborated, complex, weighty, cumulative system of thought. It holds out a precise, sophisticated and in one sense highly technical apparatus for the formulation and solution of important questions. This is supremely evident in Aquinas, whose work was immensely important for Joyce. Self-evidently, too, English and Irish Catholic tradition has beauties to rival those of revivalism. For Joyce, this was notably the case with the work of Newman, whose 'cloistral, silverveined prose' he loved (*P*, p. 179), and whom he quotes repeatedly at the beginning of Chapter 3. The trouble is that the late-nineteenth-century Irish Catholic Church was not Newman's. It was Archbishop Paul Cullen's. Cullen was Archbishop of Dublin from 1852 till his death in 1878, and Cardinal from 1867. He had a curiously double effect on the Irish Church. On the one hand, he sought to counter British influence, to create and institutionalize certain bonds between the Church and nationalism. On the other hand, even as he denounced English influences, he steadily reformed the Church in the direction of Anglo-Saxon, Protestant puritanism and Victorian English cleanliness.

It is precisely puritanical morality – a puritanical morality that, historically, was not intrinsic to Irish Catholicism, but had recently come to dominate it, partly because of English and Protestant influences – that Stephen encounters in Chapter 3. He meets it chiefly when he goes on retreat and listens to Father Arnall's sermons. Newman's disquisitions on Hell and damnation are exquisitely scrupulous and sober. Arnall's, by contrast, are crass and lurid. He sounds a bit like the eighteenth-century American puritan hellfire preacher Jonathan Edwards. Scholars have shown that Arnall derives much of the substance of his sermons from St Ignatius of Loyola's *Spiritual Exercises* and *Hell Opened to Christians* by the seventeenth-century Jesuit Giovanni Pinamonti. This is important, but should not delude us: Arnall's language, his rhetoric and imagery are vulgarly late Victorian. They draw repeatedly on Victorian middlebrow, commercial, popular-cultural and popular-scientific registers. Arnall can even sound Protestant. Not surprisingly, perhaps, one of his principal themes is the Church's colonial triumphs in distant lands.

Chapters 1 and 2 ended with personal victories that the following chapter opened up to question. The victory at the end of Chapter 3 is a strictly ironical one. Terrorstricken and oozing guilt at having sinned, Stephen flees back into the bosom of the Church. By the beginning of Chapter 4, this has lent him a seemingly profound sense of 'intricate piety and selfrestraint' (*P*, p. 154). Obedience to the Church breeds order, discipline and exactitude (including exactitude of language). Yet Stephen is uneasily aware that it does not allow him to 'merge his life in the common tide of other lives' (*P*, p. 155). By an implacable logic, the suggestion that he might join the priesthood is eventually dangled before him. At this point, however, his 'pride of spirit' rebels. A 'subtle and hostile' instinct arms him against acquiescence (*P*, p. 164). He will remain 'elusive of social and religious orders', and carve out an independent destiny for himself. 'The disorder, the misrule and confusion of his father's house' will win his soul, after all (*p*, p. 165). Thus Catholic *Bildung* gives way to *Entbildung*. Counter-formations follow in its wake. Stephen discovers his capacity for intellectual commitment. He feels 'a new wild life' within him (*p*, p. 175). He even lays hold of a 'treasure' of language that obedience to the Church had smothered (*p*, p. 170). His sense of liberation reaches its climax at the end of the chapter. Stephen gazes ecstatically at a girl in 'the likeness of a strange and beautiful seabird', standing in the water at the edge of the sea (*p*, p. 175). Here, at last, he experiences a moment of 'profane joy', and greets 'the advent of the life that had cried to him' (*p*, p. 176).

In some ways, however, Stephen sloughs off hidebound tradition less boldly than he would like to think. Yet again, he expresses his epiphany in the advanced vocabularies most immediately available to him. These stem from Catholic mariolatry on the one hand and revivalist and Late Victorian poetry on the other. Joyce steeps the bird-girl sequence in echoes of Yeats and AE. True, the literary repertoire, here, is not exactly the same as the one in Chapter 2. It is dreamy, exaltatory, rhapsodic. But it is nonetheless derivative and secondhand. In the very act of freeing himself, Stephen falls into another kind of dependency. Furthermore, the language to which he resorts, however beautiful, also holds him at a distance from the very life with which he thinks he is connecting. This helps to explain the difference between *A Portrait* and *Ulysses*. In *Ulysses*, the profanity will be very profane indeed, in more senses than one. The novel will be thick with ordinary life, and this life will be conveyed in distinctly unelevated terms.

Once more, Chapter 5 works partly as a corrective. *A Portrait* tells us a great deal about the young Joyce's moods, and their causes. But its central theme is the intellectual development described in my fourth chapter. The novel ends with an emphasis on intellect, and on the emergence of Irish modernity in the figure of a young Dublin intellectual of Catholic stock. The Stephen of Chapter 5 has grown sceptical about religion, almost to the point of urbanity. He also grows sceptical (if not without recidivist phases) about the Literary Revival, notably its absorption in Irish myth, and its commitment to a 'loveliness which has long faded', rather than 'the loveliness which has not yet come into the world' (*P*, p. 255). He is equally sceptical about the Gaelic Revival and nationalism in its present forms, not least because of their reliance on English and Anglo-Irish models of thought and feeling. Most importantly of all, whilst sceptical about the language revival, he is increasingly, deeply aware that English will always be foreign to him, 'an acquired speech', a language he cannot speak or write without 'unrest of spirit' (*P*, p. 194). The shadow of this recognition will hang over the rest of Joyce's work, in which a restless tumult seethes within the English language itself.

The Stephen of the last chapter, then, is struggling towards a modern independence, not without successes, though also not without involuntary but inevitable subservience and complicity. The struggle is not only not complete at the end of *A Portrait*: it will turn out to be never-ending. In *A Portrait*, it has scarcely begun. But Stephen's struggle for a modern independence is not principally undertaken on his own behalf. It is intended to be exemplary. He asserts his own refusal to serve. He aims to become as free and as whole as possible. He must live an unfettered life. (The image of being sprung loose from fetters recurs in Joyce's work. It is richly suggestive of a history of subjugation that would include, for example, the 'brisk traffic in Irish' to the Caribbean colonies in the seventeenth century, the Penal code of the eighteenth, Irish political prisoners transported to Australia in the nineteenth, and so on.[52]) It is clear that Stephen would want this freedom for Ireland, too. He takes himself to represent a 'race' whose type is the peasant woman of his friend Davin's story, 'a batlike soul waking to the consciousness of itself' (*P*, p. 186). Hence his closing declaration (of his determination to forge the conscience of his race).

It is here, finally, that the question of the sentimental education of Stephen Dedalus, and the obliquity with which Joyce treats it, comes in. Stephen has often been seen as altogether too intellectual, coldly remote from common humanity, in need of his complement, Leopold Bloom. But what Joyce shows us in *A Portrait* is that Stephen is by no means emotionally inert. His sentimental education happens subliminally, however, unbeknownst to himself. His mind has other tasks to finish before it can take the full weight of his experience. He must fortify himself first; that is, he must grow strong enough to bear with the historical experience of his country. It is not hard to list some relevant vignettes: the nun screeching behind the walls of the madhouse; the momentary revelation of Lynch's 'shrivelled soul' (*P*, p. 210); the feeble, half-human creature Ellen; the simian, dwarfish Scott-lover with his pathetically genteel tones; the swift decay of Stephen's athletics trainer Flynn; the strange, sad spectacle of the impoverished Dedalus children singing together for hours into the night; more largely, and perhaps above all, Stephen's brief perception, in Davin's eyes, of a residue of 'the terror of soul of a starving Irish village in which the curfew was still a nightly fear' (*P*, p. 184). Almost incidentally, but as meticulously as though he were noting the craters in shell-pocked buildings, Stephen registers the social traces of historical damage. Once again, it is melancholic work. But here, melancholy is rooted, not in any supposedly transcendent vision, but in a hauntingly desolate evocation of the historically and socially determined sadness of ordinary Dublin lives.

12

Joyce, Ireland and the War

The Joyces went from Trieste to Zurich. James and Nora had already stayed there once, on their departure from Dublin. It was in Zurich that Joyce had proudly proclaimed of Nora that 'elle n'est encore vierge'.[53] However, if Dublin and Trieste seem like eminently Joycean cities, Zurich does not. It was a Protestant city. It was surrounded by 'great lumps of sugar' (Joyce's description of the Alps, *JJ*, p. 390). Above all, it was an extremely clean city. In fact, Zurich was as jealous of its cleanliness as modern Singapore is now. When Nora dropped some litter, a policeman made her pick it up. To Joyce, the pavements of the Bahnhofstrasse seemed so clean that, if you spilt food on them, you could eat it up without a spoon. No spurts of dirty water there.

But the Zurich in which the Joyces arrived in 1915 was not the usual one. For, though Swiss and therefore neutral, it was none the less caught up in the war, since, apart from anything else, it was full of foreigners who were fleeing the conflict. In order to get to Zurich at all, Joyce had had to promise the Austrian authorities not to take the other side. This, however, he was quite happy to do. He may have still been a British subject, but he was scarcely a patriotic one. He resisted H. G. Wells's and Ford Madox Ford's suggestion that he move to England. He also turned down an invitation from the British Consulate to register for possible military service. Interestingly, he stated that the document had been sent to him in error. From the start, he behaved precisely as an

An early postcard of Zurich with its 'great lumps of sugar' on the horizon.

independent Irishman, for whom a British war was not a great matter for concern.

In refusing to accept that the British war was his, however, Joyce also sided with a specific position in the Ireland of his time. He kept abreast of political developments in Ireland throughout the war, and would have known this. Irish Unionists had massively committed themselves to the war effort, which they tended to identify with imperial values. The Irish Parliamentary Party and other constitutionalists also supported the war. Sinn Féin, however, did not. It was stoutly opposed to the imperial cause, and the war had meant that, yet again, Home Rule was on hold. The most radical nationalists were even pro-German, notably Roger Casement. They included the militant, IRB-influenced Irish Volunteers. They grew in strength as the war went on, and disillusionment with it progressively crept in.

There was no conscription in Ireland. Irish opposition to the idea was practically unanimous, and the British Government dared

A 1915 British recruitment poster aimed at Irishmen.

not risk it. The British Army's recruitment in Ireland depended on men enlisting. This they did in quite plentiful numbers, Protestants and Catholics alike. The Unionist and conservative press nonetheless repeatedly complained about Irishmen refusing to volunteer, and the Army worked hard to attract them. The propaganda campaign was intense. The posters repeatedly asserted the identity of British and Irish purposes. In effect, they restated the principle of the Union:

GRAND INTERNATIONAL MATCH
GREAT BRITAIN, IRELAND AND ALLIES
V. GERMANY, AUSTRIA AND ALLIES
ARE YOU PLAYING THE GAME?[54]

Recruiting posters repeatedly juxtaposed British and Irish motifs, the Royal Arms or the Crown with leprechauns, harps, towers and Catholic clergymen. They avoided using green and orange together, since doing so called the tricolour of Sinn Féin to mind.

From the outset, then, Joyce specifically declared himself to be one of what the *Irish Times* disparagingly referred to as the Nationalist 'shirkers'.[55] In effect, he refused the Union, agreeing with the view, shared by Sinn Féin and the Irish Labour movement, that the 'British War' was 'very little concern of ours except in so far as we are incidentally affected thereby'.[56] He was particularly contemptuous of the claim of an imperial power to be acting on behalf of small nations, and poured scorn on it in a postcard to his actor friend Claud Sykes, satirizing Lloyd George in the process.[57] As the war progressed, however, like the Irish Labour movement and even the Irish Parliamentary Party, he moved steadily closer to Sinn Féin's point of view. This was particularly the case from early in 1918, when the Military Service Bill and the spectre of possible conscription united the parties against the imposition of British recruitment practices in Ireland.

There were various factors prodding Joyce in the direction he took. Of his old Dublin friends, one, Tom Kettle, an intellectual Catholic and nationalist who had married into the Sheehy family, was killed on the Somme. Joyce clearly cared about this, if the dignified and compassionate letter he wrote to Kettle's mother is anything to go by. In the Easter Rising in Dublin in 1916, a splinter group of the IRB that was led by Patrick Pearse, and the Citizen Army, a band of armed socialists led by James Connolly, took over key buildings in Dublin, particularly the General Post Office. They proclaimed themselves the Provisional Government of the Irish Republic. This, too, had an important influence. In the Rising, Irish nationalism and Irish socialism came together. Joyce had no time for the mystical Catholicism and cult of blood-sacrifice that Pearse had espoused. But he had been sympathetic to Connolly, and was

Aftermath of the Easter Rising, 1916.

dismayed by the brutality with which the British authorities swiftly put down the insurrection, with soldiers indiscriminately killing householders. To make matters worse, when another old friend, Francis Sheehy Skeffington – a feminist and well-known pacifist who had also married a Sheehy – tried to prevent some of the looting that was going on, he was arrested, then murdered on the orders of a British officer (who later went on to become a bank manager back in England). The murder appalled the Irish public.

But there was one particular respect in which, in Zurich, to adapt a phrase of Ellmann's, Joyce found himself pitted against the British Empire itself.[58] Claud Sykes wanted to set up a theatre company, the English Players, to perform plays in English. It would make a contribution to the war effort. Joyce agreed to join him, partly because he hoped the Players would stage *Exiles*. In 1916, Prime Minister Asquith had also awarded him a Civil List grant, which did something to mollify him. It also meant he had a debt to pay, and working with the English Players would be a way of settling it, especially since the Players could put on a lot of Anglo-Irish drama (which they did; Joyce rightly thought that the best modern plays in English were written by Irishmen). At all events, implausibly enough, he took on the job of business manager.

By agreement, the amateur actors were paid less than the professionals. One of the amateurs, a British ex-soldier named Carr who worked at the Consulate, took umbrage. What happened then is instructive, and the fact that it happened at exactly the time when opposition to the war was hardening in Ireland is no coincidence. Carr had fought and been wounded and taken prisoner in France. For his part, Joyce made no secret of his own lack of loyalty to the British cause. Like Longworth before him, Carr threatened to throw Joyce downstairs. Joyce was clearly a 'green rag to a bull' (*u* 15.4497). It would be naïve to think that, in 1918, an ex-British soldier aggravated by an Irishman he took to be a coward did not resort to racist as well as personal insult. At all events, when, in Dublin's brothel quarter as evoked in *Ulysses*, Stephen Dedalus is menaced by a British soldier who is a fictional version of Carr and bears his name, Joyce was careful to capture the authentic accents of nocturnal belligerence on English streets: 'I'll wring the bastard fucker's bleeding blasted fucking windpipe!' (*u* 15.4720–21).

Joyce immediately sued Carr, partly for money Carr owed him for tickets not sold, partly for threatened assault and libel. The acting British Consul, A. Percy Bennett, quickly took Carr's side. Joyce could be fiercely litigious. He could also be quick-witted about legal matters. When Bennett, having put pressure on Sykes to enlist, tried to do the same to Joyce, Joyce complained to Sir Horace Rumbold, the British Minister in Berne, that a British Consul was inviting him to 'compound a felony' (i.e., renege on his promise to the Austrians, *sl*, p. 232). He had not obtained the 'protection and redress from the insult of violence' that he had sought (*l* 2, p. 425). Rumbold offered no support. For Joyce, there was more than a matter of law at stake. Even more than with Roberts, the row with

Carr was a question of pride and humiliation: hence the fact that, in the scene in *Ulysses*, Joyce makes Stephen not only supercilious and gorgeously articulate, but deliberately obtuse to Carr's violent rage. As with Gogarty, Longworth and Roberts on previous occasions, a personal squabble was inseparable from questions of race, class and cultural power. It was also inseparable from the question of national standing. Joyce was well aware of this, as the *Ulysses* scene again makes clear.

Once Bennett took Carr's side, Joyce stopped behaving like an independent Irishman and began to behave like a pro-German one. He praised the German offensive of July 1918 and started taking the pro-German *Zürcher Post*. He even claimed the Consulate was spying on him. In effect, during the course of the war, his position on it changed from one close to that of the Irish Labour movement in 1914 to a radical nationalist one. The process began when the representative of British power clearly and shamelessly took the English rather than the Irish side in what Joyce devoutly believed was a question of justice. In the case of Joyce versus Carr, Britain had merely identified itself with the English cause. Significantly, too, the Carr affair was winding to its end as Joyce was contemplating the shift from the comparative realism of the early chapters in *Ulysses* to the radical experimentation of the later ones.

The Carr affair continued to rankle with Joyce. But it was Bennett, Rumbold and British institutions that increasingly came to mind more often than did Carr himself. In an open letter of 28 April 1919, Joyce claimed that the Players had had 'to face calumny and detraction, disseminated by the British authorities here' (*L* 2, p. 439). He also claimed that Bennett had wanted him expelled from Switzerland 'on military and political grounds' (*L* 2, p. 440). The Consulate had persecuted him both legally and financially. When Pound heard that British government censors thought *Ulysses* was written in enemy code, Joyce not only believed him. He assumed that Bennett was responsible for the rumour. In August

1920 he was identifying Rumbold with imperial British power in Ireland. He summed up the symbolism of the whole incident in a bit of doggerel verse he sent on a postcard to Stanislaus in August 1920:

> . . . the pride of old Ireland
> Must be damnably humbled
> If a Joyce is found cleaning
> The boots of a Rumbold [*L* 3, p. 16].

In the twelfth chapter of *Ulysses*, Joyce cast Rumbold as a hangman. As late as June 1921 he was still making caustic jokes about the representatives of British power abroad. By then, however, Ireland itself was finally on the verge of independence, and its Rumbolds were in retreat.

13

Writing *Ulysses*

Joyce planned a short story called 'Ulysses' as early as 1907, though, in his own phrase, it 'never got any forrader than the title' (*JJ*, p. 230). The idea may have first occurred to him on the Mediterranean coast, but it did so at a time when he had not been long away from Dublin, and whilst he was still focused on the world of *Dubliners*. At the same time, this idea needed years by the Mediterranean to make it flower, which it did just before Joyce left Trieste. Suitably enough, on 16 June 1915, he sent a postcard to Stanislaus announcing that 'the first episode of my new novel *Ulysses* is written' (*SL*, p. 209).

Joyce wrote chapters 13 and 14 of *Ulysses* when he went back to Trieste, and the last four chapters of the novel in Paris. But it took on solid bulk in solid, bourgeois Zurich. Trieste had been raffish. Zurich was respectable. Not surprisingly, perhaps, Joyce led an increasingly divided life. He would continue to do so for the rest of his career. From the time he left Dublin in 1904, he was very careful to protect and indeed to foster an inner life that had worked loose of external circumstance. Certainly, he was much absorbed in his daily life in Trieste, Zurich and Paris. It was rich in experience and human warmth, and often eventful. He learnt a great deal from it that was important for his fiction. Nonetheless, his novels remained strangely remote from it. Unlike some of his contemporaries – Fitzgerald, Hemingway, Pound – Joyce did not turn his work into a moveable feast, relocating it as he decamped from one country to another. On the contrary, his novels were fixated on the

Ireland he had left. It is no accident that, to later friends, like Robert McAlmon, he could seem decidedly provincial.

The doubleness of Joyce's life in Zurich exactly bears out my point. On the one hand, there was the domestic upheaval of the move. The family had had to leave almost everything in Trieste, including manuscripts, papers and books. The Alpine climate meant new clothes for all. There were wartime shortages of food, including bread and potatoes. Both Joyce and Nora went through significant bouts of illness. In particular, whilst walking in the street, Joyce had an eye attack of such painful intensity that he was unable to move for twenty minutes. Nora's hair started falling out. At the same time, the sociable and convivial Joyce, Joyce the drinking man, continued to live in Zurich as he had in Trieste. He made new, sometimes cosmopolitan friends: Ottocaro Weiss, Frank Budgen, Rudolf Goldschmidt. He was a late-night regular in Zurich's cafes and restaurants. Zurich was also full of interesting expatriates, not least artists and musicians, many of whom Joyce got to know. It was home to the soon-to-be-notorious Dadaist Tristran Tzara (whom Joyce probably didn't meet) and the soon-to-be-world-transforming revolutionary Vladimir Lenin (whom he probably did).

Joyce also managed to find time for at least couple of flirtations, including one with a woman who lived across the street, Marthe Fleischmann. He claimed he fell in love with her when, in a voyeuristic moment, he saw her rising from the lavatory. He also rather cryptically claimed that Marthe eventually allowed him to explore 'the hottest and coldest parts of a woman's body'. His friend Frank Budgen assumed he had gone no further than 'fingering' (*JJ*, p. 451). At his most disreputable, Joyce not only asked Budgen (a painter) if he could bring Marthe to Budgen's flat, he even persuaded Budgen to draw a big, fat-bottomed nude for the occasion and display the picture at the appropriate time. According to Nora, he also encouraged her 'to go with other men', saying that it would give him something to write about.[60]

All this hectic, human muddle seems very distant from the almost monkish dedication and single-mindedness with which Joyce claimed to be labouring at his chosen task. In 1917, he wrote that 'as regards *Ulysses*, I write and think and write and think all day and part of the night. It goes on as it has been going these five or six years' (*JJ*, p. 416). If this is accurate, it suggests that the mental if not the physical activity of composing *Ulysses* began in 1911 or 1912. The idea of *Ulysses* was already well established in Trieste. Joyce's statement also suggests that he did not altogether distinguish between writing and thinking, inward meditation and actual composition. But how do we square the sustained intensity of focus suggested by his account – and by his claim, for example, to have spent a thousand hours on the composition of *Ulysses* 14 – with Marthe Fleischmann, nights spent drinking with Budgen and the frenetic involvements with the English Players? The answer is that what he said of Mangan was also true of himself: Ireland, its history and the pattern of his own life had 'cast him inwards, where for many ages the sad and the wise have elected to be' (*CW*, p. 55). It was from this capacity for self-enclosure, for inward withdrawal, that Joyce derived his quite extraordinary powers of concentration. Hangovers did nothing to deter him from writing. In Trieste, he completed two of the more difficult chapters of *Ulysses* sprawled across two beds in a small family home with eleven people in it. In Paris, within two months of their arrival, in the midst of a chronically uprooted life, he had managed to write six drafts of the longest chapter. The concluding chapters were partly written in an armchair with a suitcase for a desktop.

The impression of a compartmentalized life is borne out by Joyce's correspondence during this period, particularly the letters about *Ulysses*. The letters fall into four main groups: formal or business-like (as with Pound); cloying, romantic and tinged with sex (Marthe); chaffing, comradely (male friends like Budgen); and the unusual ones, the ones that, in general, Joyce seldom wrote: the personal letters. This group consists mainly of letters to one of the unsung heroines of the Joyce story, his Aunt Josephine. To compare a few of Joyce's letters to Budgen with his letters to his aunt is very revealing, particularly when *Ulysses* is (more or less directly) the subject. For the point to be quite clear, however, we need to broach the subject of Joyce and Homer.

Like Cervantes in Spain's Golden Era, Joyce was by now well embarked on a great modern national comic epic. He knew that the new Ireland needed its epic. He was also well aware of the late nineteenth- and early-twentieth-century Irish debates about the form this epic should take. He had seen these debates dominated by Anglo-Irish revivalists; but the revivalist concept of Irish epic was commonly romantic, heroic and deeply infected with images culled from a mythical Irish past. The revivalists paid scant if any attention to the Irish culture with which Joyce identified. In their conception of Irish epic, Joyce's people did not feature at all. On the other hand, various kinds of ancient epic featured in revivalist discussions of the theme, not least Greek ones. O'Grady in particular had connected Ireland with ancient Greece. Not only had he associated the Irish bards of the past with Homer. He even presented his *History* as a modern Irish equivalent of Homeric epic.

From at least 1907, Joyce, too, was interested in a modern version of Homer (though, interestingly, he was to choose the Roman rather than the Greek version of the name as the title of his novel). This modern version eventually became *Ulysses* itself, for which Homer's *Odyssey* served as a structural basis. In the first instance, Joyce was clearly concerned to counter revivalist Homeric analogies with a wickedly ironic one of his own. Beyond that, he was enthusiastic for the Homeric analogy in *Ulysses* as advertising his own epic intentions. Furthermore, he had learnt from his difficulties with Richards and Roberts on the one hand, and Pound's enthusiasm for his work on the other. He increasingly thought it might be prudent to play up what Pound had called the Homeric scaffolding of the novel. For the scaffolding was a very large part of the appeal of *Ulysses* to its most significant early readership. It gave them purchase on what all too easily looked like a formidably difficult if not unreadable work. This was important, since the early readership was the one that would ensure the novel's initial survival.

Joyce's letters to Budgen have been a standard point of reference for critics. That is partly because they modernistically emphasize the 'specially new fizzing styles' of the later chapters of *Ulysses* (*SL*, p. 245). But they also make the Homeric analogy sound like the key to the book. Budgen had been a sailor. Joyce clearly felt that the Homeric material in *Ulysses* would interest him. It might even encourage Budgen to promote the novel (and indeed, Budgen duly wrote one of the most influential, early books on Joyce and *Ulysses*). Aunt Josephine didn't write a book. She was Joyce's mother's sister. What we know of her suggests an 'intelligent, resourceful and unfailingly generous' woman, in Ellmann's phrase (*JJ*, p. 20). She was Joyce's favourite aunt. He saw her as 'the wise woman of Drumcondra' (*JJ*, p. 213) and confided in her. She was also a crucial source of Irish material for *Ulysses*, and he constantly pestered her for information, newspapers, magazines and books.

The letters he wrote to her while composing the novel are ravenous for exact detail, much of which he undoubtedly used. Can she tell him whether the Star of the Sea church is visible from the seashore? Are there steps leading down at the side of it from Leahy's terrace? Are there trees in the terrace itself? Is it possible for an ordinary person to climb over the area railings of 7 Eccles Street and lower himself down on the other side? He also wanted inexact detail: gossip, rumour, stories taken from the popular press. Can she give him the gossip about the Powells and the Dillons? He wants all the information she can get, both tittle-tattle and fact, about the maternity hospital in Holles Street. Can she send him novelettes and a penny hymnbook, a gazette or police news from the newsagents, a copy of *Reynolds's* or *Lloyd's Weekly News* or the *News of the World*?

These are sometimes confused with scholarly requests, as though what lay behind them was primarily Joyce's need to fit some tiny pieces of inert matter into his vast new modernist jigsaw puzzle. Actually, what they speak of is love, or obsession, or both together. Whether he was wholly aware of it or not, he was repeating Columcille's habit of 'longing thought' in a foreign land. The tone of the letters to Aunt Josephine is not always wholly kind. But it is a tone of ordinary, domestic intimacy. The same kind of shared intimacy with a small world is clear enough in all Joyce's enquiries about Dublin. True, he told Aunt Josephine that, to understand *Ulysses*, she needed to read the *Odyssey* first. Even his favourite aunt was not exempt from a lesson in epic purpose. But his last letter to her, after he had heard that she was seriously ill, is one of his few genuinely loveable ones. Joyce's struggles with language were normally intellectually and politically motivated. The news of his aunt, he said, simply left him too shocked for words. He nonetheless wrote of his gratitude, affection and respect. Right to the end, however, he stressed what he and Aunt Josephine had in common: a stock of memories, a fund of mundane Irish lore. He shared the scaffolding of *Ulysses* with Budgen. He shared its substance with his aunt.

14

The National Epic

Joyce began *Ulysses* almost immediately after finishing *A Portrait*. This deepens what might seem to be one of the abiding mysteries of his career: how did he get from the one vision to the other? The two novels are both performances of sublime virtuosity. But they are written in radically different modes and seem to work to very different ends. The dominant tone in *A Portrait* is carefully balanced between the cool, intellectual detachment of the vivisectionist and a melancholy often not far from bitterness. By contrast, *Ulysses* is, above all, a comic novel. It bubbles with irrepressible laughter. This laughter is by turns mocking, satirical, philosophical, political, blasphemous, transformative, humane and inhuman, compassionate and cold, dirty and extremely dirty. It is many other things, too. In a moment of inspired perception, Yeats described Joyce as having 'a cruel playful mind like a great soft tiger cat'.[61] Much of the humour in *Ulysses* is clearly the product of such a mind. Like Puck with Shakespeare's mechanicals, the maker of labyrinths everywhere teases and taxes his readers, toys with them, misleads, distracts, puzzles and befuddles them. In a phrase of George Meredith's that is crucial to *Ulysses*, the reader must be made to incur the '*immense debtorship*' for the '*thing done*' (*U* 9.550–51). Joyce wanted to exact from his readers, said Philippe Soupault, 'an effort matching his own' (*PE*, p. 117). Thus reading becomes a kind of atonement: atonement, that is, for the sombre history that is pervasively and tightly woven into the very stuff of the novel, and without which it would have been unthinkable.

In the end, Joyce's transition from the muted world of *Dubliners* and *A Portrait* to the gleeful play of *Ulysses* and *Finnegans Wake* cannot be attributed to external factors. Whatever its advantages to the Joyces in 1915, the move from Trieste to Zurich was hardly a move to a warmer and more cheering environment. The transition in Joyce's work has a purely meditative, inward and aesthetic logic. Not surprisingly, it is chiefly traceable, not to the circumstances of Joyce's life, but in his work itself. Joyce carries Stephen Dedalus over into the first three chapters of *Ulysses*, in which he is the central character. He also deepens Stephen's melancholy. For the Stephen Dedalus at the beginning of *Ulysses* is obsessed with history, as his earlier self was not. The history in question is Irish in the first instance, though other histories are drawn into its orbit, by way of the long-established Irish habit of thinking of history and politics in terms of analogies. Soupault thought Joyce endured a 'fecund suffering' of the memory (*PE*, p. 112). Certainly, history shakes Stephen's imagination like an ague. He casts its fitful, tumultuous onsets in a language of the most exquisite beauty. But this can only mitigate, not allay its power to haunt him. By contrast, Mulligan pleads the cause of historical amnesia ('Look at the sea. What does it care about offences?', *U* 2.231); Haines the Englishman offers an emptily formal acknowledgment of historical guilt whilst enthusing over the romantic curiosities of Ireland's 'Celtic' culture. Deasy applauds the triumphalist narrative of Ulster Protestantism and relishes the promising new turn it appears to be taking. It is hardly surprising that, alongside these three, Stephen appears morose and unamiable; or that Joyce dresses him 'in cheap dusty mourning' (*U* 1.570–71).

Stephen does not surrender inertly to the power of history. As he says himself, if history is a nightmare, it is one from which he is trying to awake. Joyce aids and abets him. At the end of *A Portrait*, he had started to break Stephen up, registering his experience as a series of disconnected diary entries. He takes the process a stage further in *Ulysses* by resorting to the so-called 'stream of consciousness' technique (which actually tends to make consciousness judder more than stream). This has the effect of fragmenting and dispersing our impression of Stephen's character, making it seem open to possibility. Stephen himself meditates on history as 'an actuality of the possible as possible' (*u* 2.67). But, though Aristotle lies behind his terms, Stephen's abstruseness partly gives the game away. Joyce was inexorable. 'Stephen', he said, 'has a shape that can't be changed' (*jj*, p. 459). Stephen's struggle with his nightmare is in vain. In truth, historical actualities are 'fettered and branded' and 'lodged in the room of the infinite possibilities they have ousted. They are not to be thought away' (*u* 2.49–51).

At this point, however, after the first three chapters, Joyce engineers a radical shift in *Ulysses*, indeed, in his whole thought (for Joyce's art is a form of thought). Enter the modest and unpretentious figure of Leopold Bloom. Bloom is an advertising canvasser whose father was Jewish and whose mother Irish. He is therefore not strictly Jewish himself, though others invariably think of him as a Jew. It is his experiences and the 'stream' of his consciousness during the morning of 16 June 1904 that occupy most of the next five chapters. Though other things start to happen to *Ulysses* after Chapter 8, on the realistic, everyday level, Bloom remains the central character. He is the reader's version of Ariadne's thread. No one has evoked the complexity of an ordinary life, of a basically cheerful, sane, resilient, flawed, ordinary city-dweller's mind, better than Joyce does in Bloom.

Here several features need emphasis. First, whatever the personal significance to Joyce of 16 June 1904, it is significant for Bloom because it is the day on which his wife first commits adultery. (Critics have quarrelled about this, but it is almost certainly the case.) Bloom knows the adultery will take place. He even knows more or less exactly when. The knowledge threatens to unsettle his psychic balance. *Ulysses* charts an intricate process in which this balance is alternately made precarious, restored and repaired. At the very core of the novel, then, is the question of how to come to terms with betrayal. Joyce was obsessed with betrayal. He was obsessed by it in personal, historical and political terms. In gloomier moments, he tended to think of Ireland as a country of betrayers, its history as punctuated with significant treacheries, and its political cause as having been repeatedly scuttled by one traitor or another. Again and again, he returns to the idea that the sin in which the pathology of colonial Ireland originated was Devorgilla's adultery. Joyce was hardly a full-blown allegorist. Indeed, he was deeply distrustful of the consequences of too much allegorical thought, certainly as far as the health of Irish culture was concerned. Part of him disowned the allegorical mindset. But steeped as he was in Catholic intellectual tradition and, above all, in Dante, allegory was part of his inheritance. He was not inclined to wish that inheritance away. He thought allegorically too, often in profound and subtle ways. He precisely understood the implications of writing a modern novel about a stranger being allowed into an Irish house and a modern Irishman's need to accept unfaithfulness. He may even have seen Molly Bloom as putting an end to the parenthesis that (he thought) had begun with Devorgilla.

It is important to recognize that, for Joyce, Bloom is a modern Irishman. Throughout the novel, Dublin men who are at best blinkered and insensitive, at worst frankly anti-Semitic, call Bloom Jewish rather than Irish. But Bloom is not an instance of that disconcertingly uniform phenomenon, the modern European Jew. Though he is interested in Zionism, he has been quite thoroughly assimilated, which means being given a local and specific (Dublin-Jewish) identity. More often than not, Bloom's knowledge of Jewish beliefs, customs and practices is hazy and unreliable. When quizzed on his nationality, he firmly asserts that he is Irish. This is crucial to Joyce. Whatever his sympathies with Arthur Griffith and Sinn Féin

A Dublin Jewish family in the early 1900s.

– and, to a more limited extent, with D. P. Moran and *The Leader* – Joyce was stoutly opposed to their disastrously narrow conceptions of Irish nationality. He knew that their lapses into bigotry were a logical consequence of colonial Irish history, not least, of a racist habit of thought whose origin was English and went back at least as far as the Tudor invaders. But he also knew that, for Ireland to liberate itself properly from its history, it had to liberate itself from such consequences. In effect, he says that through Bloom. Bloom shows us what Irish modernity might mean. He also shows us how far Joyce's Ireland still had to go properly to reach modernity.

Bloom's personality also reveals what Joyce thought was lacking in Irish culture. Bloom is even Joyce's paradigmatic modern Irishman. He represents a direction in which Ireland needed to turn. In his ordinary, pedestrian central character, Joyce presents an image for the Irish future. Bloom is even a utopian figure. Joyce locates him solidly where he belongs, amongst Dublin Catholics. Bloom spends most of his time in the midst of this community, and it looms much larger in his mind than does Dublin Jewry. In their own mild but distinctive way, Bloom's politics are also the politics most evident in the Catholic community: pro-Parnellite, anti-imperial, sympathetic to nationalism. But at the same time, he is a non-Jewish Irish Jew who has been baptized as both a Protestant and a Catholic.

When asked why Bloom, Joyce replied that only a foreigner would do. Bloom is both intimate with and foreign to the Dublin culture fashioned by the two imperial masters. It is the culture he knows best. But he has neither the intimacy nor the complicity with it that stems from historical disaster and profound hostility to the conqueror. This means that he can serve as an extremely subtle and flexible instrument of critique. For Bloom, colonial structures turn out to be a source of perplexity, common-sense surprise, amusement or just indifference. His reflections on them repeatedly take place at a liberating distance. So, too, he is close to his Catholic acquaintances, but also estranged from them. As a Jew, Bloom comes from a people who have known oppression, misery and catastrophe. Unlike Joyce's Dubliners, however – and pointedly unlike Stephen – when the thought of historical desolation threatens to overcome him, he swiftly bounces back: 'Morning mouth bad images. Got up wrong side of the bed. Must begin again those Sandow's exercises. On the hands down' (*U* 4.233–4). Through Bloom, Joyce partly identifies with the interests of the Catholic community. But he also points to the limits of its political and cultural ambitions and its stifling obsession with the retrospective view. In doing so, he develops an intricate, composite politics of his own.

Joyce uses Bloom, then, to turn Dublin inside out, to make it familiar and unfamiliar together. He uses him to show the constraints colonial Irish culture imposes on the character and independent development of his Dubliners. Having set this process going, however, Joyce seems increasingly to have felt that he had to double it. Bloom is a man of average education. He has only a limited experience of colonial Irish institutions and institutional discourses.

He also has only a very limited knowledge of Irish Catholicism. These very limits are partly what make him such a useful weapon against Church and state. But they also restrict his scope. Joyce had to open up a second front. In the most general terms, this front is linguistic. In *A Portrait*, Stephen had described his soul as fretting in the shadow of the English language. With the partial exception of Chapter 7, however, it is only from the ninth chapter of *Ulysses* onwards that the struggle for freedom also clearly becomes a seriously linguistic struggle.

The famous styles in the second half of the novel have attracted a great deal of attention as supposedly modernist *tours de force*. In fact, Joyce generated them out of his struggle with England and Rome, and the long history of their domination of his country. He usually chooses a contemporary English or Anglo-Irish discourse or verbal structure as a basis for a style. He may put this discourse together with others, or with a Catholic one. He then 'treats' it (or them). Each chapter thus subjects a discursive complex to a set of artistic practices. These practices are remarkably varied. The most obvious one is parody. For much of the time, however, Joyce does not just imitate familiar discourses in order to ridicule them. He takes forms of English writing, or Catholic forms, like the catechism, and subjects them to distortion or wickedly misuses them. He twists them to ends that are not their own. He writes back at them, and over them. The styles in *Ulysses* have usually been thought of as great modernist achievements that sprang from abstract ideas. In fact, they are more like extraordinarily brilliant specimens of graffiti work. In the second half of *Ulysses*, Joyce was partly scribbling over a set of massive but oppressive old monuments that were rapidly approaching their sell-by date.

This is not clear in Chapter 10, though Chapter 10 continues the process of the formal and linguistic break initiated in Chapter 9. Chapter 10 provides a conspectus. It takes what Stephen calls 'a look around' (he is quoting Parnell, *u* 10.827); that is, it scans the city of

Dublin itself, at a particular time of day. Stephen is pausing on the threshold of a momentous decision, of departure and commitment to his Irish art. So, too, the novel itself pauses and surveys the scene before embarking on the political and aesthetic project that constitutes its second half. From Chapter 11 onwards, however, while the plot moves forward, it also has frequently to be dug out of the Joycean word-pile. In Chapter 11 itself, the style is allegedly musical. It would be better to call it quasi-musical, since what the (very musical) Joyce actually does is to use the idea of music to warp and even brutalize the English language, to bend it out of true.[62] There is a particular point at stake in this: the Anglo-Irish revivalists had dreamt of an 'ultimate reconciliation' of the English language and the essential Irish spirit as supposedly represented by music.[63] Joyce will have none of this artificial union. He insists on and multiplies our awareness of cacophony, radical discord. Music is reconciled with English only at the price of English itself.

The next six chapters work in similar ways. Chapter 12 takes revivalist historiography as its basis. Chapter 13 puts sentimental, late-nineteenth-century Irish Catholic mariolatry together with the treatment of gender in London's popular press (women's magazines in the first half of the chapter, low-to-middlebrow English newspapers in the second). The staple of Chapter 14 is Victorian and Edwardian anthologies of English prose. Through its treatment of these, the chapter also strikes at the 'Whig version' of literary history. This made of English literature a single, unbroken, racially determined tradition stretching from King Alfred to Kipling. Chapter 15 is about 'the unconscious'. Strictly speaking, more than anything else, it is about the Dublin unconscious, and the English habits that lie buried at every level of Dublin minds. The main point of reference, here, is not writing but speech. Chapter 16 is concerned with the idea of 'proper English'. The progress of this idea had accelerated during the Victorian and Edwardian periods, very much to the prejudice of marginal or disempowered groups (colonial peoples,

the Irish, Scots, Welsh and Cornish, Cockneys, provincials etc.).
In Chapter 16, Joyce makes great art out of defiant impropriety,
putting together a gorgeous and ingenious tissue of blunder, sole-
cism and error. The basis for Chapter 17 is 'imperial science', British
science as advanced and promoted, at the end of the nineteenth
century, to preserve Britain's commercial position, and with it,
the Empire.

If Joyce's verbal practices in the second half of *Ulysses* can be
summed up in one word, it is adulteration (which of course fits
exactly with his real-life theme). He everywhere takes the discourses
of the two masters and gleefully poisons and corrupts them. He
injects them with what they would hope to exclude, above all, ordinary Irishness (as opposed to the Yeatsian-romantic kind). Colonial
cultures are 'hybrid' cultures: that is the contemporary view. Joyce
was certainly well aware that Irish culture was irredeemably mixed
and impure. But his art does not merely passively register the fact.
In an awesomely powerful gesture, he takes hold of hybridity and
masters it. However critical of Ireland he could sometimes be, Joyce
was profoundly convinced of what he called the 'ignobility' of the
powers that had overcome it (*cw*, p. 75). Merely to note the fact of
hybridity was therefore unambitious; to rail at it, even more so.
Joyce sought rather to reverse the vector of colonial power. He did
to the invader what, for centuries, the invader had done to Ireland:
he denied his autonomy and contaminated his purity. Adulteration
was a form of work. In undertaking it, Joyce placed his art at the
service of those the imperial masters had excluded from power.

It is thus that *Ulysses* becomes a national epic. The novel is
saturated in a consciousness of Irish history. But its sophisticated,
subversive work is also very much of its time. The two – historical
consciousness and contemporary work – are intimately related. Joyce
knew he was writing for an Ireland on the brink of independence. In
principle, *Ulysses* was the great new cultural document of a liberated
nation. But the liberation it offers itself is pervasively ambivalent,

shaded, compromised. A free Ireland cannot immediately or perhaps ever be quite free of the monstrous historical shadows that dog it. Furthermore, Joyce's work of adulteration paradoxically triumphs over colonial history only by confirming it in place. The irony of that is central to *Ulysses*, and Joyce is very much in command of it. It means that, as a national epic, *Ulysses* must and can only be comic. Stephen himself knows, not only that he must learn to 'kill the priest and the king' in his mind (*u* 15.4436–7), but that he must laugh 'to free his mind from his mind's bondage' (*u* 9.1016).

For all its undoubted and at times ferocious aggression, *Ulysses* is thus also very much about resignation, acceptance, settling for things. This emerges above all in the last chapter, which is wholly made up of the thoughts of Molly Bloom as she lies in bed, early in the morning of 17 June. Joyce said that the word 'yes' with which the novel ends signified 'the end of all resistance' (*jj*, p. 712). His chapter is about this in two senses: the aim of resistance, which is to challenge, subvert, overthrow and maybe even transform the power resisted; and the conclusion of the process, which is reconciliation with the effects of that power. It is surely no coincidence that he was writing his last chapter in 1921, the year of accommodation in Ireland. It saw the negotiation of the Anglo-Irish Treaty and the truce between the IRA and the British Army. The truce was signed on 7 July, more or less as Joyce was planning Molly's chapter.

Joyce knew what he was doing when he gave his last chapter to a woman. The Irishwoman's point of view – Irishwomen's culture – has either been absent from *Ulysses*, or relegated to second place within it. The second-class status mirrors women's place in the Dublin the novel evokes. With Molly, however, Joyce overturns this hierarchical relation. He understood very well that Irishwomen stood in relation to Irishmen rather as Ireland had so long stood in relation to England. If the one structure of power was to disappear with independence, then so should the other. That a woman finally comes to the fore in the Irish national epic as written in 1921 is

Arthur Griffith entering Downing Street in 1921 to negotiate the Anglo-Irish Treaty.

quite obviously significant. Yet, so, too, are the attitudes of this particular woman. Molly is caustic about the imperial British militarism with which she grew up in Gibraltar. But she is equally scathing about Irish Catholic and nationalist masculinity, not least because of its penchant for fatal violence. Indeed, she is well aware of how far Irish mirrors English bellicosity even as it claims to be rootedly opposed to the British imperium. By contrast, she herself is at ease with her own contradictions. She is irritated by the British, with their 'damn guns bursting and booming all over the shop' (*U* 18.679–80). But she surrenders her Irish lover's Claddagh ring to an English soldier. Through Molly, in fact, Joyce insists on the value of a relaxed anti-imperialism that is not automatically and in principle based on an unswerving allegiance to nationalist orthodoxy.

15

Monsieur Joyce in Paris

Joyce quit Trieste for the second time in 1920. He arrived in Paris on 8 July. It is important to note that he did not originally intend to settle there at all. Paris was supposed to be just a staging post on the way to London. Imperial capital or not, by 1920 living in London made a lot of sense. Having masterminded the publication of *A Portrait*, Pound had also arranged for *Ulysses* to be serialized in the *Little Review*, an avant-garde journal in Chicago and New York (though he was a little worried by the first real evidence of what he called Joyce's 'arsthetic' obsession, *JJ*, p. 442). He had managed to generate a great deal of excitement about Joyce in London, with writers from Wells to T. S Eliot, Katherine Mansfield and Virginia Woolf all taking an interest.

Harriet Shaw Weaver was in London, too. Harriet Weaver was a reticent and extremely decent Englishwoman with a capacity for genuine and humble admiration. Her background was genteel and rather staid, but she had an independent and adventurous streak (feminist, communist, supporter of avant-gardes). She had taken over the editorship of what soon became the *Egoist* in 1914 and brought out the first full English edition of *A Portrait* in 1917, after its initial publication in New York. She also found a London printer willing to print some of the episodes of *Ulysses* for inclusion in the *Egoist*. She had money, and often spent it on good causes. Luckily for Joyce, she decided to make him one of them. By 1917 the Joyces had become financially quite reliant on her. She continued to support them for the rest of Joyce's life. She even paid for Joyce's funeral.

Interest in Joyce there may have been in London, but it was not always enthusiastic, or even kindly. Pound himself saw Joyce's art as rising above his Irish origins to achieve international status on the modern, European scene. But Joyce's English and Anglo-Irish reviewers tended to see him very differently. They were more inclined to read him in terms of three related themes: class, race, and sex or obscenity. Joyce's writings were squalid, dirty, unpleasant, coarse and bad-mannered. This was hardly surprising: Joyce was Irish, and unregenerate Irish, too, as was his subject matter. Virginia Woolf called him ill-bred. Others claimed that he was trying to run down the language and aiming at the very heart of English tradition. Alfred Noyes thought he was out to depreciate 'the value of some of the noblest pages in our literary history'. S.P.B. Mais accused him of literary Bolshevism. Most tellingly of all, as we saw earlier, Shane Leslie asserted that *Ulysses* was a Fenian attack on the institution of English literature.[64]

Perhaps it was as well, then, that Joyce chose Paris not London. But this, again, was partly due to Pound. For Pound, too, was in the process of transferring his own activities to Paris, having despaired of London. He helped find the Joyces a small, three-room flat in Passy. The 16th arrondissement was not a bad spot from which to launch a masterwork. Just round the corner, as he boasted himself, Balzac had floated the *Comédie humaine* upon a sea of coffee. But the Joyces did not stay in Passy long. They moved again, and again. Though they were to remain based in Paris for nearly twenty years, they did not exactly settle there. In Louis Gillet's phrase, Joyce 'continued wandering between Passy and the Gros-Caillou, Montparnasse and Grenelle, not counting the escapades, the eclipses, the letters which without warning showed him to be in London, Folkestone, Basel, Copenhagen' (*PE*, p. 167). However, if legend has associated Joyce with Left Bank bohemianism, in fact,

Joyce and Pound in Paris, 1923, with Ford Madox Ford and John Quinn.

he and Nora increasingly hankered after a degree of bourgeois respectability and comfort. Friends and acquaintances in Paris quite often thought of him as a faintly conservative and old-fashioned figure.

Paris was good to Joyce. He met Sylvia Beach, owner of the bookshop Shakespeare and Company on the rue Dupuytren. She became the publisher of *Ulysses* when it turned out that no regular publisher would take the risk, and remained one of Joyce's most important props until 1931, when they fell out over business and money matters. Sylvia Beach also introduced Joyce to Valéry Larbaud. Larbaud was one of France's foremost exponents of English literature. He read the *Little Review* numbers, and pronounced himself 'raving mad' over *Ulysses* (*JJ*, p. 499). The French public must hear about this book. As soon as *Ulysses* was finished, he would give a public lecture on it. Larbaud was a very literary man. He saw at once that Joyce had claims to being a modern

Rabelais. But he was also astutely conscious of the temper of the times. Comparisons with Rabelais were hardly likely to be the best way of promoting *Ulysses*. Larbaud's talk rather linked Joyce with Einstein and Freud. It announced that the key to *Ulysses* was the *Odyssey*, and stressed the extraordinary complexity of its structure and the Jewishness of the hero. The modernist *Ulysses* was born. It was very different to the *Ulysses* that had outraged Noyes and Mais.

Promotional tactics were very much the point. Joyce knew that his way to the English-speaking world was partly through French criticism. Furthermore, Larbaud, of course, was right. In a postwar climate distrustful of stuffy old tradition and eager for innovation, it was the modernist *Ulysses* that people wanted; and not just French people, either. In the 1920s, Paris was not only a city of avant-garde artists and intellectuals. It attracted them from many different parts of the world. Joyce got to know Hemingway and Djuna Barnes. T. S. Eliot and Wyndham Lewis came to visit him. The man who had written *Ulysses*, which had challenged so many conventions, and was soon working on *Finnegans Wake*, which challenged still more, became a luminary, lodestar and iconic figure. Admirers rang his doorbell and climbed on chairs to get a glimpse of him.

Joyce was well aware that he could turn the public furore to his advantage. Hardened by his encounters with Richards and Roberts, since the Zurich years he had become much shrewder not only about how to publicize his work, but where and to whom. Eric Bulson has recently shown that, as early as 1917, Joyce was 'pulling the strings' of those writing the first articles about him in Trieste. He asked Harriet Weaver to solicit reviews from Italian newspapers and journals. 'I would do all this myself', he told her, 'but it is difficult to push one's own wares'.[65] Better to encourage his willing helpers to push them. Herbert Gorman, Stuart Gilbert, others: Joyce gradually recruited an increasing number of friends and associates to the cause of his work. However, though they wrote books about him, or it, or both, in reality, they functioned less as interpreters or acolytes than a PR team, if, admittedly, a various and not always wholly reliable one.

As Bernard McGinley puts matters, if Joyce 'was committed to his art', he 'knew the value of multiple truths and multiple selves in promoting it'.[66] According to his friend Soupault, he was 'immensely delighted' by the efforts others made to explain him, 'especially when they were furthest from their aim' (*PE*, p. 115). His teasing way with exegetes is clear from the collection of essays about *Finnegans Wake* over which he later presided, *Our Exagmination round His Factification for Incamination of Work in Progress*. He stood behind his 'twelve marshals', he claimed, telling them 'what lines of research to follow' (*JJ*, p. 613). But the 'marshals' were at best idiosyncratic, and the inclusion of two light-hearted 'letters of protest' conveys an exact sense of how seriously he took the project. Joyce had an acute understanding of historical processes. He was well aware of the auspices under which he would best be promoted. He was also well aware of their historical contingency. The reference to ware-pushing is crucial. Joyce was careful to guide others' accounts of his work. But he was not aiming to get things right for posterity. He was more concerned to ensure that posterity should read his work at all. This meant 'spinning' it for the modern European scene.

For modern Europe was scarcely equipped to receive an extraordinarily complex and subtle vision of Ireland, its history and colonial agonies, its present and future hopes; still less so, a vision steeped in Irish lore and learning. The very framework for thinking about Joyce like this did not emerge for several decades. Even today, in spite of the shift in thought exemplified in 'postcolonial studies', such receptivity is fitful at best. Yet those who knew Joyce in the Paris years tend repeatedly to stress two things about him. Firstly, there was the singleness of purpose, the intense dedication which increasing fame did nothing to diminish. Secondly, there was what

Nino Frank called Joyce's extreme 'mental privacy' (*PE*, p. 78). Soupault remarked that those incapable of even imagining what lay behind Joyce's 'perpetual slavery' often mistook his remoteness for egotism (*PE*, pp. 10 8–9). But some understood it exactly. Frank was one of them: 'the principle of Joyce's personality' was that 'he had roots in a place' (*PE*, p. 79). He was nourished by an 'indestructible' bond 'with the land that was the source and sustenance of his artistic personality' (*PE*, p. 97). Ole Vinding recalled Joyce telling him that 'every day I get papers and other news from home' (*PE*, p. 146). Non-Irish friends remarked, not just on how often Irish friends came to see him, but on the fact that that Joyce treated them as newsbearers.

'While Joyce the exile wandered from town to town', wrote Louis Gillet, 'on the shores of the Tiber or the Adriatic, on the quays of the Seine or the banks of a Swiss lake, he was – like Ulysses – a dreamer in search of Ithaca, and living only in his fatherland' (*PE*, p. 169). Stephen Dedalus's recollections of Kevin Egan in Paris can by no means be straightforwardly applied to the Joyce who found himself there nearly twenty years later. It is nonetheless worth recalling, again, the power with which Stephen evokes a life spent obsessed by a country oblivious, not just to one's obsession, but to one's longing to see it transformed. Ireland might have forgotten Joyce, not he it: 'Remembering thee, O Sion' (*U* 3.264).

16

Joyce and Free Statehood

But while Joyce was completing *Ulysses*, Ireland was becoming a different place. Independence seemed possible again, if within certain limits. Then the country began to come apart. In 1912 the increasingly hardline Protestant and Unionist majority in Ulster had declared against the Home Rule Bill, with the enthusiastic support of equally hardline Unionists in Britain. This led to the formation of the private army known as the Ulster Volunteers, and plans for a provisional government in Ulster. In the south, nationalists responded by setting up their own army, the National Volunteers, not least with the idea of forcing Ulster to accept Home Rule. When the Irish leaders in parliament committed the Volunteers to the British war effort without condition, a more radical, IRB-influenced group broke away. They called themselves the Irish Volunteers. The Easter Rising was one consequence of this. From the Rising emerged a new, broad-based Sinn Féin, and a leader who would turn out to be the *eminence grise* of Irish politics for much of the next 60 years: Eamon de Valera.

De Valera rapidly became President of Sinn Féin and the Irish Volunteers. In 1919 he also became first President of the alternative Irish Parliament, the Dáil Éireann. The British duly declared it illegal. De Valera went on the run. The years 1919–21 saw the Anglo-Irish war, conducted between the British troops and police and the Volunteer extremists who now called themselves the IRA. Chief amongst the British forces were the notoriously thuggish police

Cork city centre after its firing by British Auxiliaries in 1920.

reinforcements known as the Black and Tans and 'Auxies', whose
tactics, like sacking townships and burning down part of Cork city
centre, were sometimes grimly reminiscent of Cromwell's. Joyce
was acutely aware of what was going on: as his Aunt Josephine
informed him, 'there's nothing but raids and murders here'.[67]
Meanwhile, gallingly for nationalists, the Government of Ireland
Act set up a parliament and an administration in Ulster. It opened in
June 1921. The Partition of Ireland had become an established fact.

By 1921 both sides in the war could claim advantages, but
both were also at a disadvantage. The British Army in Ireland was
severely stretched, not least because the enemy's tactics were
masterminded by the redoubtable Michael Collins. The IRA was
now being massively bankrolled from America. However, it was
also losing men and arms. Britain was coming under international

pressure. More importantly, the question of Ulster had (in one sense) been settled. The British could now afford to negotiate with nationalist Ireland. The time was ripe for a truce. The Treaty of 1921, however, turned out to be yet another historic misfortune. The trouble was that Lloyd George offered Ireland only dominion status, which left it as part of the Empire. De Valera and the Dáil were willing to agree to the Ulster question being settled by a Boundary Commission. They were even willing to let the British keep their naval bases. But they insisted on being free of the British Crown. Ireland – or most of it – had to become a republic. De Valera even produced an alternative to the Treaty, 'Document no. 2', in the hope of fitting Ireland into what would soon be known as the British Commonwealth without compromising on the republican question. In *Finnegans Wake* Joyce would make much of this.

As Joyce said in 1929, 'that blackguard Lloyd George knew what he was doing' (*JJ*, p. 610). The Irish representatives signed the Treaty and it was ratified in the Dáil, if by the slimmest of majorities. But Ireland then rapidly split between pro- and anti-Treatyites (or 'irreconcilables'). De Valera resigned as President of the Dáil and formed an anti-Treaty party. In January 1922 the first government of the Irish Free State took over from their British overlords in Dublin Castle. The triumph was short-lived. The IRA split, part of it (the 'Irregulars') opposing the Treaty, part of it turning into the army of the new State. As so often in post-colonial cultures, the immediate legacy of a long history of colonial domination was horror, bloodshed, internecine strife. The Ireland divided by Partition was riven all over again by civil war. A culture so deeply scarred by barbarities inflicted in the name of a supposedly superior civilization was hardly likely to produce its own fully modern civilization overnight. The fissure between political realists and exalted, intransigent visionaries snaked its way though organizations, communities, even families. It was sometimes complicated by older hostilities and feuds. The result was not just armed conflict, but assassinations, executions without trial, arbitrary and casual reprisal. In Yeats's phrase, the nightmare rode upon sleep.[68]

Joyce had always thought that Ireland was inclined to tear itself apart, not least when on the threshold of victory. He was distinctly unimpressed by the Civil War. When Aunt Josephine told him, Yeatsianly, that most Irish people now seemed to have got 'a hardening of the heart', he replied, 'It seems so: and a softening of the brain' (*SL*, p. 293). He had reason to be mordant: if Ireland was always in James's thoughts, Nora had been hankering after the real thing. In 1922, in spite of Joyce's urgent attempts to dissuade her, she took the children, first to Dublin, then to Galway. As it happened, de Valera was in Galway at the same time, speaking against the Treaty. A few days later, anti-government forces seized the warehouse opposite the Joyces' lodgings. Free state troops promptly invaded their bedrooms and planted machine guns at the windows. Nora, Giorgio and Lucia escaped on a train which was then caught in an exchange of fire between troops on board and rebels along the line. They had to lie down to avoid the shooting. According to Joyce, 'when Nora's uncle heard the story of her sprawling on the floor and the rale old Irish bullets hopping off the promontory of her back he nearly fell off his chair laughing' (*SL*, pp. 293–4). But Joyce himself was not amused. Indeed, the strain of events was such that, once his family were safely back in Paris, he promptly collapsed with a furious eye attack. When, early in 1922, the Irish Minister of Information asked him if he would come back to a newly independent Ireland, Joyce had tersely replied, 'Not for the present' (*JJ*, p. 534). The Galway incident seemed to confirm that he had been right.

Joyce's reluctance to return to Ireland was only deepened by the development of William Cosgrave's Irish Free State from the Civil War to the election of de Valera's Fianna Fáil party in 1932, and indeed Ireland's development after that date. For the Free State remained strikingly unfree. Hence the fact that Joyce could imagine

'Eireweeker to the wohld bludyn world' (*FW*, 593.3): Eamon de Valera's first broadcast after victory in the 1932 election.

an Irish republic incorporating Ulster and beyond the reach of English power, and yet remain indifferent to the prospect: 'any semblance of liberty they had when under England seems to have gone', he remarked, in 1932, 'and goodness knows that was not much' (*JJ*, p. 643). The Free State became preoccupied with defining itself in terms of a native, indigenous, Gaelic culture and its alleged historical grandeur. This also meant defining Irish in stark opposition to English culture. The compulsory teaching of the Gaelic language became law. So did the required use of it in official public life. But the new culture was not only one of what Yeats called 'enthusiastic Gaeldom'.[69] It seemed that 'the Catholic conscience alone must dominate Ireland'.[70]

Alas, this 'conscience' did not in the slightest resemble either Joyce's, or the one he had hoped to forge. It was not saturated in a rich awareness of Catholic literary, intellectual and historical traditions, and had – to say the least – no truck with heresy. The 'Catholic conscience' of the new Ireland was a comparatively shrunken one. The Free State was profoundly suspicious of corrupting foreign influences. It took the moralism and xenophobia which, as Joyce had pointed out in *Ulysses*, Ireland had partly inherited from Victorian and Edwardian England to stifling extremes. It was vigorously opposed to all traces of sexual irregularity, from birth control to advertisements for cures for gonorrhoea. It came very close to legislating formally against divorce, and the divorce bills drawn up stood *de facto*. In 1937 de Valera's new Irish constitution finally made them law. But, from an Irish artist's point of view, perhaps the most dispiriting feature of Ireland after independence was its vigorous commitment to censorship. A censorship bill became law in 1929. By 1935, when Samuel Beckett wrote an essay on the theme, he was able to state that there were 618 books and 11 periodicals on the Irish Register of Prohibited Publications. Proscribed authors included Shaw, O'Casey, George Moore, Austin Clarke, Maugham, Aldous Huxley, D. H. Lawrence, Faulkner, the Powys brothers, Boccaccio, Casanova, Jarry, Colette, Céline and West (Mae). Joyce himself would posthumously join the list, with *Stephen Hero*.

Beckett found a metaphor for the situation in a crop whose modest success was one of the few meagre signs of economic progress in the new Ireland: 'We now feed our pigs on sugarbeet pulp. It is all the same to them.'[71] But if the censorship bill meant cretinization, it also spelt political oppression by other means. For the bill made it possible for old Civil War enemies to deny each other freedom of speech. In any case, from mutiny and murder in the Free State Army in 1924, through IRA violence, attacks on property and jury intimidations in the '20s, to IRA threats against 'Free Staters' in 1929 and after the 1932 election, the legacy of Civil War conflict, bitterness and extremism was never far from the surface of Irish life. By a strange, unhappy but seemingly inexorable logic, a 'free' Ireland seemed to be replicating the very forms of historical outrage to which it had so long been subjected. Meanwhile, the Catholic imperium merely tightened its grip.

By 1932 Joyce was describing Ireland not only as a country he 'did not dare to go to', but one 'where not three persons know me or understand me' (*SL*, p. 360). Failure of comprehension was very much the point: from a Joycean point of view, Ireland was either misconstruing the nature of the struggle with the two masters, or refusing properly to engage in it at all. Joyce amply recognized the oppressive features of the new culture. But he also recognized the repressions as symptoms of persistent weakness. Ireland remained a country of 'poor sick people' and 'poor priests, consolers of these last' (*SL*, p. 373). Irish people were showing too little of Stephen's strength of will, Bloom's resilience or Molly's vitality and sense of proportion. All the same, he was not about to relinquish old positions. Thus, after the 1932 election, Yeats and Shaw proposed to set up an Academy of Irish Letters. They did so partly to counter the Catholic exclusivism that loomed ever larger in Ireland. When Yeats approached Joyce to get him to join, however, Joyce refused. So, too, ten years earlier, he had asked Lady Gregory to omit 'all mention' of himself from her history of the Irish literary movement (*SL*, p. 290). He may have despaired of the Irish classes with whom his own interests were most closely identified. But he was not about to be co-opted into a social and cultural elite increasingly concerned to set itself above the Catholic hordes. After all, in the eighteenth century, the Protestant Ascendancy had done precisely that.

17

Joyce Enterprises

On 11 March 1923 Joyce wrote to Harriet Shaw Weaver: 'Yesterday I wrote two pages – the first I have written since the final *Yes* of *Ulysses*' (*JJ*, p. 551). By 6 June he was reading 60-odd pages of his new work to Valery Larbaud. He had embarked on his last and what for most people, scholars and ordinary readers alike, is his most obscure and perplexing book, *Work in Progress*, as it was known until it was nearly finished, when it became *Finnegans Wake*.

The *Wake* was composed in a very different fashion to Joyce's earlier work. Joyce was now a celebrated modern genius surrounded by admirers. He was ruthless in using this situation to his advantage. If he had assembled a promotional team for *Ulysses*, he now also put together his own support unit. According to Stuart Gilbert,

> he got people to put their time – and sometimes money – completely at his disposal; to follow him wherever he wanted them to accompany him: boring plays and operas, dull expensive restaurants; to [cancel] their agreements if he wanted their assistance in some trivial, easily postponed task; to run errands for him, pull strings for him, undertake delicate and distasteful missions which exposed them to snubs, rebuffs, and ridicules at his bidding.[72]

Gilbert was an Oxford-educated Englishman who had formerly been a judge in colonial Burma. He may have fancied himself an arbiter in matters of fair and honourable conduct (an irony Joyce would have relished). The Irishman with the cruel, playful, tiger cat mind probably took a little pleasure in turning Gilbert into Boots. There was none the less a kernel of truth in Gilbert's general observation. Joyce increasingly became Joyce and Company, of which he none the less remained executive director and sole inspiration.

This was particularly the case with the *Wake*. Joyce's relationship with the Jolases is one example. Eugene and Maria Jolas were Americans, though Eugene's parents were from Lorraine. They had founded an avant-garde review called *transition*. They became key figures in the new entourage. Joyce decided to publish extracts and drafts of the *Wake* serially with them, beginning in 1927. In the long term, this was to have major consequences for its reception, in which an understanding of it as a formidably hermetic, definitively abstract, modernist *tour de force* has always predominated. Another figure who became practically indispensable was Paul Léon, a wealthy Russian émigré who was devoted to Joyce and effectively came to serve as his (unpaid) personal assistant and secretary. Together with the Swiss architectural historian Sigfried Giedion and his wife, art critic Carola Giedion-Welcker, the Jolases and Léon formed the core of the Joyce circle in the 1930s. By contrast, Sylvia Beach and even, in the long run, Harriet Shaw Weaver became less important. Pound was no longer in Paris, and had faded from the scene.

Joyce might seem to have exchanged Left Bank bohemianism for a less louche and abandoned, more professional set of companions. But in another way, as always, he continued to live in two worlds. For all his reluctance even to set foot in the Free State, his less glamorous ties to Ireland not only remained many, varied and deep, but also became more outward ones. Joyce might publicly claim to be unwanted and unnoticed by his own people. In fact, to a much greater extent than in Trieste or Zurich, Ireland came looking for him. Old friends from the days before exile, some of whom had been fictionalized in *A Portrait*, like J. F. Byrne, Padraic and

Mary Colum, Hanna Sheehy Skeffington and Constantine Curran, all made their way to Paris at different times. So did members of Joyce's and Nora's families, like Stanislaus and Michael Healy. Dubliner Patrick Tuohy painted his portrait (and his father's). Younger Irish writers and poets like Thomas McGreevy, Brian Coffey and Arthur Power came to see him or were drawn into his orbit. Most significantly of all, the young Beckett attached himself to Joyce. As a writer, Beckett both learned profoundly from and reacted astringently against Joyce's example. Like a number of other members of Joyce's circle, he worked both as an amanuensis and a researcher for *Work in Progress*, reading books at Joyce's behest and reporting back to him.

To a greater extent than at any time since he had left, in conversation at least, Joyce was once more saturated in Ireland, particularly Dublin, in their literature, history and geography. He and his Irish friends talked endlessly about particular Irish people and places. He steeped *Work in Progress* in both. He listened to Radio Éireann, or Radio Athlone, as he preferred to call it, hearing Irish voices through static and foreign interferences, as does the reader of the *Wake*. (Ironically enough, the station's call-sign was '2RN', suggesting that listeners 'come back to Erin'). Joyce remained an astute self-promoter during the 1930s. But he saw self-promotion as his way of promoting his country. If the growth of Joyce tourism in Ireland is anything to go by, he was right to do so. Increasingly, he promoted Ireland in Europe in other, usually small and typically idiosyncratic ways. In this respect, he did his duty by the Free State, though on his terms, not its.

He became particularly interested in promoting the Irish tenor John Sullivan. Like Joyce's father, Sullivan was a Cork man. Like Joyce himself, he had long been living in continental Europe. Stanislaus met him first. He recommended Sullivan to his brother, who was soon enthusing about Sullivan's voice. Sullivan claimed to be struggling against Italian domination of the operatic scene.

Joyce quickly identified their two causes. He roused his friends. He urged them to attend Sullivan's performances, at which he himself would shout 'Bravo Cork!' (*JJ*, p. 621). He got them to write on Sullivan's behalf or review him in the papers. He approached Sir Thomas Beecham, via Nancy Cunard, Lady Ottoline Morrell, via Wyndham Lewis, and the Irish High Commissioner in London. He even tried to persuade George Antheil to write an opera for Sullivan.

In a tribute entitled 'From a Banned Writer to a Banned Singer', Joyce paired himself together with Sullivan. There is a good deal of Wakean wordplay in the piece, so it's easy to miss much of the point. 'From a Banned Writer to a Banned Singer' was published in *The New Statesman and Nation*, with an introduction explicitly asserting that Joyce's complaint was that Sullivan was '"banned" or at least unknown in England' (*cw*, p. 346). But the complaint was also an account of the logic of Joyce's own continuing self-banishment. By the 1930s, this logic included the Anglo-Irish war, the Civil War and the progress of the Free State. Joyce takes a swipe at the old invader, notably Cromwell ('gentlest lovejesus as ever slit weasand' (*cw*, p. 214). He no doubt had the Black and Tans partly in mind. He even ends the piece by having the three Italian tenors whom Sullivan suspected of conspiring against him give a mock-rendition of the British national anthem. He scoffs at the venality of the Church ('as only roman as any *puttana madonna*', *cw*, p. 213). But, as in *Ulysses*, he also aims at Catholic exclusivity ('O.u.t. spells out!') and the Catholic (as opposed to the Protestant) will to persecution: 'Get ready, get ready, scream the bells of our Lady. And make sure they're quite killed, adds the gentle Clothilde' (*cw*, p. 214). The orchestration of the St Bartholomew's Day Massacre to the tune of London's greatest nursery rhyme might seem trivial and tasteless. But Joyce was clear-eyed: in Ireland, violence amongst Catholics was confirming in place the very habits of oppression from which, at long last, a Free State had notionally declared its independence. In a culture apparently unable swiftly to surmount its historically induced recidivism, neither he nor Sullivan were likely to find a place.

Joyce and Sullivan were once photographed with the Irish writer James Stephens. Joyce suggested that the picture be captioned 'Three Irish Beauties'. Stephens was another Irishman whose interests, in a sense, Joyce promoted: indeed, in a rather astonishing interlude, he considered promoting Stephens to the position of co-author of the *Wake*. Joyce had first met Stephens in Dublin in 1912. Unpromisingly, Stephens had later described Joyce as 'a disappointed, envious man' (*JJ*, p. 334). This view, however, was not to survive their next meeting, in Paris. Joyce and Stephens had the same first name, and had both been born in Dublin on 2 February 1882. According to what Joyce told Stephens, they had also been born at the same time, 6 a.m. Joyce had read some of Stephens's (emphatically Irish) work, and liked it. He himself was tiring of his labour on the *Wake*. Might Stephens not take it over? This at least was what Joyce proposed, in a letter to Harriet Shaw Weaver:

> Of course he would never take a fraction of the time or pains I take but so much the better for him and me and possibly for the book itself. If he consented to maintain three or four points which I consider essential and I showed him the threads he could finish the design [*SL*, p. 323].

This might seem like a mildly unbalanced idea. In fact, it bears witness to what Joyce saw as the extreme impersonality of his work. If Stephens were to shoulder the burden of the *Wake*, he wrote, 'it would be a great load off my mind' (ibid.). The book made its own demand. It had to be written, no question of that. But if writing the *Wake* was a responsibility, it was becoming an onerous one. Why not have someone else finish it, since Joyce had already laid down all the guidelines? And who better than another Irishman with exactly the same span of biographical and historical experience of

Ireland and Dublin, their culture and their language, their recent hopes and disappointments? In fact, Joyce's interest in Stephens was motivated by the same concern for historicity or extreme historical specificity that had been so evident in *Ulysses*. It was also motivated by what were still epic intentions.

Stephens was later to praise Joyce for one of his most conspicuous virtues, and another one perhaps less obvious: 'you are the most subtil man, and the most continuously kind male creature I have ever known' (*JJ*, p. 696). Nothing came of Joyce's plan to raise Stephens to a perhaps rather dubious glory as the man who completed *Work in Progress*. It was hardly likely that anything could have come of it. But the episode helps us understand a little of what Joyce's conception of *Finnegans Wake* might have been. It also helps us recognize how desperate his life was becoming.

18

A Wild, Blind, Aged Bard

In the *Wake* – or what Joyce called his *'funferal'* (*FW* 120.10) – there is a sentence that has often seemed to encapsulate an aspect of its author's later life: 'Loud, heap miseries upon us yet entwine our arts with laughters low' (*FW* 259.7–8). Miseries there were indeed. Joyce seems to have had a rather strange constitution, part-robust, part-vulnerable and febrile. His biggest problem was his eyes. These had always been weak. He had serious trouble with them in Trieste. Then, in 1917, he had his eye attack in Zurich. An operation followed, but he was repeatedly plagued with attacks of iritis, to the point where, in 1921, he needed five weeks' rest and a great deal of cocaine to recover from one of them. By 1922 the problem was very much worse, with glaucoma threatening, as it had in Zurich, and one eye blood-filled. He had arthritis, too. He even had a mouthful of rotten teeth that needed extraction. If *Ulysses* is a reliable guide, they may well have been decaying untreated since at least 1904. By 1923 he was claiming that his eyes were no longer strong enough to read the work of others. He was operated on again in the summer of 1924, and again, later in the year, and again, in the spring and winter of 1925 and the summer of 1926. The round of consultations and operations continued in the 1930s. By 1934 a neighbour noted that Nora had to put the milk and sugar into Joyce's tea. He could no longer go on walks, and started to carry a white cane. He used a white dinner plate for an ashtray. He seemed to be living in a crepuscular world. When Harriet

Shaw Weaver mentioned sunlight, he asked her, 'What is it like?' (*JJ*, p. 571).

He said that his work on the *Wake* sometimes left him 'literally doubled in two by fatigue and cramp' (*JJ*, p. 598). César Abin captured the curvature in question when, for Joyce's fiftieth birthday, he drew him as a question mark. Joyce often had stomach trouble. He also had trouble with his daughter. Since the family had arrived in Paris, Lucia had enthusiastically trained as a dancer, and had had some small success. She decided, however, that she did not have the strength to make dancing her career. She had long been close to her brother, Giorgio. His love affair with Helen Fleischman, whom he married in 1930, left her ill at ease. She had rather unsuccessful relationships with a number of men, including Beckett. By the late 1920s she was showing signs of depression. In February 1932, on Joyce's fiftieth birthday, she turned on her mother in rage and threw a chair at her. A few weeks later she had a catatonic episode. Thus began a years-long sequence of crises, scenes, furies, hysterias and panics, flights from home, doctors and psychiatrists, hospitals and clinics, injections and operations, more or less dubious 'cures' and appeals for help to long-suffering friends. Lucia spent time in various different sanatoria in France and Switzerland. She became Jung's patient, for a while. She went to London, where she wreaked havoc in Harriet Weaver's life. She went to Ireland, where she had a similar effect on family, friends and relatives. Joyce was anguished, indulgent and impractical. He alternately credited Lucia with startling powers of insight and took her mental disorders to be intimately related to his own gifts. He refused to see her as incurable or to have her certified, though, from 1936, he had to accept that she would spend her life in institutions. Just for good measure, in 1938, his daughter-in-law Helen also suffered a mental breakdown.

There were times when the upheavals in Joyce's own life seemed one with the monstrous political lunacy increasingly gripping

Europe. On occasions, he cast himself as a man of sorrows, as in his list of the Joycean days of the week, or what Louis Gillet called his 'almanac of Jeremiah': 'Moansday, Tearsday, Wailsday, Thumpsday, Frightday, Shatterday' (*PE*, pp. 198–9). Once, in a lavatory, having made sure no one else was there save an Irish friend, he screamed extremely loudly, and at length; to which the friend responded, 'Look, that'll be enough now, do you mind?'[72] Through all his misfortunes, however, Joyce's dedication to his work remained unstinting. *Work in Progress* mirrored his plight: 'It is night', he said of it. 'It is dark. You can hardly see' (*PE*, p. 233).

In Joyce's case, however, even the sufferings of age formed part of a tradition. As is clear from *Ulysses*, the young Joyce had some-times imagined himself as a modern version of the Irish bard. It was the older Joyce, however, who most came to resemble one. Joyce was not principally a poet, but then, the ancient Irish bards were not just poets, either. Many of them were powerful officials attached to the court of a king or chieftain. They were law-givers, chroniclers and genealogists. Depending on the bardic order to which they belonged, they were learned in fields like law, music, history (and pseudo-history) that loom very large in *Ulysses* and the *Wake*. They were also legendary satirists, much feared by the powerful. Joyce repeatedly expressed the conviction that Ireland ought to be listening to him. This might seem arrogant, vain and even slightly mad. But it was also a bardic conviction. In asserting it, Joyce was refusing to surrender an ancient and peculiarly Irish version of the idea of the Irish artist as the legislator of his people.

The bards survived historical vicissitude from pre-Christian times to the early nineteenth century. As invasion followed inva-sion, however, bardic poetry changed. In the words of eighteenth-century scholar Joseph Walker, 'the sprightly Phrygian gave way to the grave Doric'.[73] Panegyric, rhapsody and lampoon yielded to incitements to revolt. According to Edmund Spenser, the bards notoriously glorified disobedience, licentiousness and insurrection.

Not surprisingly, Henry VIII and Elizabeth I passed laws against them. The bard Nelan was said to have been the spark that ignited Thomas Fitzgerald's rebellion against Henry VIII. Even more than a poetry of revolt, however, bardic poetry also became a poetry of lamentation, in which personal and political grief were repeatedly mingled. The figure of the bard became inextricably associated with suffering on the one hand and complaint on the other.

Many of the later bards call Joyce to mind: they were often blind, itinerants and drinking men, frequently on the move, dependent on the generosity of those who recognized their importance: the eighteenth-century Cormac Common, for example; Turlough O'Carolan, who sought to cheer and sustain the Irish through the dark times of the Penal Code, and the picture of whose sightless face the young Joyce would have encountered as the frontispiece to George Sigerson's *Bards of the Gael and Gall*;

Turlough O'Carolan, 'The Celebrated Irish Bard', frontispiece to George Sigerson's *Bards of the Gael and Gall: Examples of the Poetic Literature of Erin* (1897).

Doncad MacConmara, who composed a mock-heroic Irish *Aeneid* long before Joyce wrote his mock-heroic Irish *Odyssey*; and Anthony Raftery, the last of the bards, who died as late as 1835. The older Joyce seems to have liked quoting from Yeats: 'Be you still, be you still, trembling heart'.[74] He might equally have quoted Féilim McCarthy's well-known *caoiné* or lamentation-piece: 'In the narrow house of pain I lie/Thrice racked with woeful misery'.[75] Yet the abiding impression of Joyce in his fifties is not one of chronic distress. He was usually resilient and creative in the face of adversity. He also laughed a lot. Here, too, he was bard-like.

Yet again, there seems to be a curious and significant order to chance and coincidence in Joyce's life. So, too, with the completion of *Finnegans Wake*: this time, however, the logic at stake was that of an endgame. Joyce finished the *Wake* late in 1938, in spite of stomach cramps. It appeared on 4 May 1939. Four months later, war was declared. Lucia was in a *maison de santé* in Ivry, outside Paris. Joyce was anxious lest she be left alone in a city – he thought – about to be bombarded. She had to be moved. Giorgio and Helen Joyce were now living apart. Helen underwent another breakdown, and was also hospitalized. Joyce and Nora left Lucia for Paris again. But Parisian life and lives were rapidly changing. People were now abandoning the city at a great rate. By Christmas, the Joyces – James, Nora, Giorgio and grandson Stephen – were all in Saint-Gérard-le-Puy. Joyce was lugubrious and racked with abdominal pains. Village life made him listless, and he worried about Lucia. He ate poorly. There were days when he seemed so exhausted that Nora thought she would lose him. Urged by friends, he planned to reach Zurich, and spend a second war in neutral Switzerland. This, of course, was difficult to do, particularly since Joyce wanted to take all his family with him. When he applied for visas and permission to stay, initially, the Swiss authorities did not recognize his name and – by a nice irony – took him for a Jew. In December 1940, however, the family finally made it, minus Lucia. By then, however, Joyce was ill. He died at 2.15 a.m. on 13 January 1941, of a perforated ulcer and peritonitis. As Nora understood, others would have to keep his indomitable spirit alive. When a priest asked her if Joyce should not have a Catholic funeral, she replied, drily, 'I couldn't do that to him' (*JJ*, p. 742).

19

The Megalith

Finnegans Wake is a unique achievement. It has comprehensively
baffled and frustrated those who have tried to come to terms with
it. It has also created its own particular band of aficionados, the
'Wakeans'. They form a distinct group within the Joyce community,
and their esoteric knowledge can be formidable if not forbidding.
The problem with the *Wake* is that one cannot, in any ordinary
sense, read it. It is composed in what seems, initially at least, to
be a singularly intimidating language of its own. This language
harbours traces of more than 60 live and dead languages. It bristles
with recondite allusions. Commentators have devoted much time
and effort to digging a story out of the *Wake*. They have dilated
on the characters who supposedly throng it. But every version of
the narrative is disputable. There are clearly shadowy figures in
the book that have names and symbolic functions. But it is hard
to trace them, or to separate them from one another with any
great certainty. Joyce himself asserted that 'there are, so to speak,
no individual people in the book' (*PE*, p. 149). It had no 'goahead
plot' (*L* 3, p. 141). Faced with such a lack of the usual incentives,
it is not surprising that readers have tended to wilt. If they keep
going, the news that the book is a vast elaboration of a particular
modernist aesthetic, philosophical case or theory of language can
easily seem, not only a scant consolation for their effort, but a
questionable one. If the point in the end is an abstraction, why
not read the criticism rather than the text? Why did Joyce need

Inscribed stone at the entrance to Newgrange, Co. Meath, the most famous Irish megalithic site.

to make the point in exactly this way, at such length, and at such immense cost to himself? Why did he bother at all?

Joyce's friend Nino Frank provided a more arresting answer to these questions than most. Joyce's last book, he remarked, is 'a sublime work; a megalith . . . like those at Carnac or Easter Island' (*PE*, p. 103). Frank may have been unaware of Irish megalithic culture (cromlechs, dolmens, menhirs, passage-tombs). But Joyce was not. Like Irish megaliths, *Finnegans Wake* is a massive, strange, cryptic construction with embellishments that defy interpretation. It might be thought of as having a partly funerary purpose. It serves as both an encyclopaedia and a memorial, a prodigious testimony to the life and history of a people. However, there are three obvious objections to Frank's analogy. The first is that megaliths become obscure through time. There is no reason to assume that they were obscure to the culture that produced them. But what if the culture were obscure from the start? What if, for centuries, it had been dominated by an alien power, which had driven it underground, if not annihilated it? Joyce wanted to commemorate a subjugated culture. He also wanted to write a sense of its historical invisibility into the commemoration itself.

The second objection is more or less automatic, for Joyceans: surely the *Wake* is distinguished by its universality or, more fashionably, its internationalism? Otherwise, what are all those other languages doing there? Why the vast and eclectic range of cultural reference? As I said in Chapter 1, the 'internationalist' reading of Joyce has been precisely determined by historical and political factors, particularly the long dominance of international modernism and postmodernism in Joyce studies. These factors have encouraged the habit of reading the *Wake* centrifugally rather than centripetally. Strip them away, as time will certainly do, and it is clear that Ireland is as much the predominant focus in the *Wake* as Florence is in the *Divine Comedy*. The range of reference to Irish materials in the book – Irish topography, geography, mythology, Irish lore and literature, Irish historiography from Giraldus Cambrensis to Standish O'Grady and John Gilbert – vastly exceeds other kinds of reference. If there are characters, events, scenes, landscapes and cityscapes in the *Wake*, they are consistently Irish at root. Whatever the limits to a concept of 'setting' in the *Wake*, no one has ever claimed that it is set in Paris or Trieste. Of course, the 'internationalists' are by no means altogether wrong: the non-Irish material is hardly unimportant. But, from the start, it is drawn into an Irish orbit and made to signify in an Irish context. If historical circumstance, political oppression and economic need repeatedly drove Irish emigrants and refugees out into the world, Joyce makes the world come trooping to Ireland.

The third objection is the strongest one: *Finnegans Wake* is clearly about much more than historical memory. It is keenly responsive to contemporary culture, from cartoons to the telephone, radio and even early television. It is also a prophetic text, a meditation on the future, particularly the Irish future. If it is a monument, then, it is a very unusual kind of monument. Here again, though, the fact that it deals with a specifically colonial history is crucial. A monument to a colonial history risks fixing in place an image of disaster, defeat and despair. It is a monument to the victories of others. Joyce's solution is to combine Irish history with a thought about actual and possible change in Ireland and an Ireland open to the world. The title *Finnegans Wake* suggests remembrance, commemoration, a testimony to the power of the past. It also suggests an injunction to a new start or entry into a new 'free state' (Finnegans, Wake!). The book holds these impulses together. In this way, it exemplifies the 'coincidance of contraries' (*FW* 49.36), a lesson Joyce said he learnt from the sixteenth-century Italian philosopher Giordano Bruno, whose work is important in it.

It is worth stressing four particular features of the opening section of the *Wake*. The first is the evocation of an age-long history (and indeed mythology) of internecine violence. This is delivered in a tone of childish pity and awe, as if beyond the limits of comprehension:

> What clashes here of wills gen wonts, oystrygods gaggin fishy-gods! Brékkek Kékkek Kékkek Kékkek! Kóax Kóax Kóax! Ualu Ualu Ualu! Quaouauh! Where the Baddelaries partisans are still out to mathmaster Malachus Micgranes and the Verdons catapelting the camibalistics out of the Whoyteboyce of Hoodie Head. Assiegates and boomeringstroms. Sod's brood, be me fear! Sanglorians, save! Arms apeal with larms, appalling. Killykillkilly: a toll, a toll [*FW* 4.1–8].

The principal points of reference, here, are clearly Irish: Malachy II and Brian Boru, for example, were rival pre-Conquest kings. The 'fishygods' are the prehistoric Formorians who battled the Tuatha de Danaan, called 'oystrygods' because Gods of the west ('ouest'),

Galway in particular, famous for its oysters. Most fancifully, though not without point, Joyce pits the de Verdons (an Anglo-Norman family going back to the Conquest) against the Whiteboys, the agrarian insurrectionists whom Joyce's great-great-grandfather was reputed to have joined. Like Stephen at the beginning of *Ulysses*, the *Wake* will repeatedly slide back into the nightmare of Irish history. This can seem like a retaliatory spiral, as is poignantly the case with the Anglo-Irish War. When Joyce writes, for example, of 'the reducing of records to ashes, the levelling of all customs by blazes' (*FW* 189.35–6) he accuses the British Army and republicans together. The specific reference is to the capture in 1921 of the Customs House in Dublin by the Dublin Brigade of the IRA. This was intended to strike at the heart of the British administration in Ireland and hasten the end of the war. In fact, it sparked off a ferocious counter-attack that led to the destruction of the building by fire. Certainly, the violence in question in the *Wake* is by no means simply the violence involved in the colonial devastation of Ireland. It is present in the history of other invasions. It shows in tribal warfare and internal Irish squabbles. The *Wake* pervasively testifies to a split and fissured culture, most obviously, perhaps, in the bickering pairs and divided couples that throng its pages, and whose archetype is fratricidal strife.

The second important feature of the first section of the book is its reference to a monumental principle that is the antithesis of Joyce's own. If there is a monument that is particularly significant in the *Wake*, it is the Wellington monument in Phoenix Park in Dublin. The *Wake* takes us on a tour of a museum or 'museyroom', an imaginary, crypt-like space located under the monument itself. The tone is ribald if not scathing:

This is the big Sraughter Willingdone, grand and magentic in his goldtin spurs and his ironed dux and his quarterbrass woodyshoes and his magnate's gharters and his bangkok's best

An early postcard of Phoenix Park, Dublin, showing the Wellington Monument.

and goliar's galoshes and his pulluponeasyan wartrews. This is
his big wide harse [*FW* 8.17–21].

The monument was not just a tribute to the 'Iron Duke'. It was also
an assertion of British imperial triumph within the Irish capital.
Here, however, Wellington's name functions as a vortex attracting
miscellaneous allusions to warfare with which he had no connection (the battles of Magenta and Golden Spurs, Goliath, the
Peloponnesian War). Part of the comic point is to displace the references to Wellington's actual victories that adorn the monument
itself.[77] Joyce also conflates the Irish with Wellington's Indian and
French opponents on the battlefield, relentlessly taunting the
British imperial hero.

The British colonial presence in Ireland is everywhere stamped
on the *Wake*. The royal visits of Henry II in 1171, George IV in 1821
and Edward VII in 1903 are among the most obvious examples. But
the Wellington monument is also a sign of historical complication.

It is a stark image of a compromised national identity. The fictional museyroom is a preliminary indication of how far the *Wake* will be concerned, not just with the traces of the historical invader, but with Irish involvement and complicity with him. For Wellington had himself been born in Ireland, of aristocratic, Ascendancy stock. As a young man he served as aide-de-camp to the Irish viceroy and held the family seat in the Irish parliament. Later, as British prime minister, in one of his very few political (as opposed to military) successes, he actually worked extremely hard for Catholic emancipation.

It is interesting to note that, not surprisingly, the IRA shared Joyce's distaste for imperial monuments. But where they actually blew up Nelson's Pillar on O'Connell Street (in 1966), Joyce is content to deface the Wellington monument with Wakean graffiti. The legacy of the colonial past was not to be abolished at once. The Wellington monument continues to loom large over the *Wake*. Against this emphasis on the grip of history, however, we should counterpoise the third and fourth features of the beginning of the book, the figures of the builder, and the giant interred beneath Dublin or in the Irish landscape. Both of these will intermittently appear throughout. The first is connected with the founding and building of the Irish capital. But he is also linked to the idea of rebuilding it, of the beginnings of a new national and civil life. Like Blake's Albion, the second is an image of a lost, buried, radically different conception of what the nation might possibly be. Neither figure, of course, is entirely without reference to the past. But both imply its creative redemption. They represent a different way of thinking about Irish history to the museyroom.

The four 'characters' who wander through the *Wake* as Mamalujo represent another way of thinking about the Irish past. They are evidently meant to make us think of the Gospels. But Joyce's 'four-bottle men' are also 'analists' (*FW* 95.27). The principal reference, here, is to the *Annals of the Four Masters*. The *Annals* constituted the last great historical achievement of indigenous Gaelic culture in Ireland, before its cataclysmic defeat in the seventeenth century. To many Irish minds, they were therefore shrouded in melancholy. In the nineteenth century, however, they were appropriated by Anglo-Irish antiquarians. Joyce makes Mamalujo sound like both Gaelic historians and Trinity College professors. He also makes them comically forgetful, and their discourse repetitious, windy, self-contradictory, inaccurate and error-strewn. In effect, they are an instance of burlesque history. Through Mamalujo, Joyce lightens the burden of Irish history in travestying and even deliberately trivializing it.

I have by no means exhausted the strategies Joyce adopts in the *Wake* in relation to the problem of Irish history. The mysterious letter is another one. It is partly an expression of revolt, as indicated by its provenance (Boston, Massachusetts) and its addressee (the English king). But it also enters the book as a missive from the past to the future, sent in the aftermath of wholesale destruction. Again and again, Joyce returns to the question of breaking with, writing and rewriting, accepting and resisting history. Of course, there is more than one imperial presence at stake in this: *Finnegans Wake* repeatedly conflates Church and state power, as in the fable of the Mookse and the Gripes. It also recognizes the continuation if not the deepening of the intimate conspiracy between the two in the new Ireland: '*Pardon the inquisition, causas es quostas? It is Da Valorem's Dominical Brayers*' (*FW* 342.10–11). So, too, the grim hold of the Church on the Irish imagination is a pervasive theme, principally in the idea of sin. As the *Wake* returns obsessively to historical violence and oppression, so too it does to sin, rumour, gossip, accusation, self-exculpation, commandments and prohibitions. To this, Joyce playfully but profoundly opposes the idea of the *felix culpa*, the doctrine of the fortunate fall, the glad acceptance of evil done, not least because of its work for the good.

The idea of the *felix culpa* is significant for the politics of the *Wake*, its ethics, and its historical thought. However, there was little hope that either the Free State or de Valera's Ireland would glimpse the wisdom of it. Joyce was partly concerned with the question of a new Ireland. Was it really possible? Was it even desirable? If either, or both, how, how far, and in what circumstances? The beginning of the final section of the book opens at dawn, a classic political trope in what was known as Irish 'sunburstery'. It is strewn with references to the first fifteen years of the Free State and what Joyce elsewhere calls 'the devil era' (*FW* 473.8):

> Array! Surrection! Eireweeker to the wohld bludyn world.
> O rally, O rally, O rally! . . . The smog is lofting . . . Sonne feine,
> somme feehn avaunt! [*FW* 593.2–9]

Eire issues its rallying-call to the whole bloody (and whole Dublin) world, echoing the patriotic toast 'Sinn Féin Amhain!' ('Ourselves Alone!'). Yet the ironies rapidly accumulate. The new Ireland may conceive of itself as autonomous, separate, pure ('Kilt by kelt shell kithagain with kinagain', *FW* 594.3–4). The *Wake*, however, is fiercely satirical about this. The idea of a Gaelic nation is backward-looking, retrograde and narrowly ethnocentric. In any case, de Valera's deeply Catholic constitution has a distinctively British stink about it, as Joyce suggests by playfully referring to its 39 articles. The sequence also mixes nationalist slogans promiscuously with British advertisements, suggesting the continuing commercial and, to some extent, even ideological dominance of the (immensely) greater power. The more the new Ireland emerges, the more it appears to be slipping back into the old Ireland.

This is reflected in the treatment of two more 'characters', the brothers Shem and Shaun. Joyce associates Shem with himself, with art, creativity, sex, vitality, laughter or 'joyicity', debt and drink. Shem is the Irishman exiled or in flight from Ireland. He is subjected to intense if sometimes light-hearted critique, notably in *Finnegans Wake* 1.7. Shaun is, above all, the Irishman in Ireland.

He is associated with the bourgeois virtues, industry, seriousness, self-denial, abstinence and thrift. After a somewhat chequered career, he is eventually called on to take his place at the head of the new Ireland, only promptly (and in Joyce's terms parodically) to turn it into a Catholic and nativist triumph:

> Oyes! Oyeses! Oyesesyeses! The primace of the Gaulls, protono-
> torious, I yam as I yam, mitrogenerand in the free state on the
> air, is now aboil to blow a Gael warning [*FW*, 604. 22–4].

As town crier, papal Protonotary Apostolical and Primate of both Gauls (Celts) and Galls (foreigners), Shaun announces a 'free state' that sounds worryingly one-dimensional.

The *Wake* repeatedly twists and turns around questions of release from and relapse into historical patterns. It treats these questions in many different and subtle ways. Not surprisingly, Joyce was interested in theories of historical repetition. This was particularly the case with Giambattista Vico's historical account (in *New Science*, 1725) of human evolution in terms of cyclical repe-titions, *corsi* and *recorsi*. However, Vico was a monarchist enthusi-astic for ideas of empire, and there was much in his thought that Joyce didn't take altogether seriously. Yeats was important, too. In 1926, in *A Vision*, he published his own cyclical theory of history. Throughout the 1920s and '30s, he grew increasingly committed to such thinking. In Yeats's case, however, it was retrospective, nostalgic both for Ascendancy culture and an imagined heroic past. Thus 'The Gyres' tells us, for example, that 'A greater, a more gracious time has gone', but that 'all things' will run 'On that unfashionable gyre again'.[78] Yeats's 'vision' was increasingly conservative. Joyce counters the Yeatsian version of historical cycles with a Catholic alternative. But he presents this alternative playfully and ironically. Such a presentation allows him to explore the idea of historical repetition, not as a consolation for the disappointments of the present, but as an extremely complex and difficult problem. In *Finnegans Wake*, the problem of repetition goes hand in hand with the question of progress.

If the title *Finnegans Wake* has more than one meaning, so had Joyce's provisional title. *Work in Progress* was both a labour and a study in the cause of modern Irish progress. At one and the same time, Joyce was producing a cultural history, a complex account of the newly 'independent' Ireland, and a reflection on its possible future. *Finnegans Wake* is acutely aware of how far the historical British presence continues to make itself felt in an Ireland that boasts of having escaped its clutches. The new freedom is more rhetorical than real. But if the *Wake* is conscious of the problems of Ireland after independence, it is also overwhelmingly conscious of their historical origins. In fact, it is driven by two equal and opposite forces: the will to resist Irish history, and thereby surmount it, and the will to come to terms with it, spelling resignation and acceptance. On the one hand, the colonial experience is profound and ineradicable. On the other hand, the *Wake* everywhere works not to obliterate but to transform the colonial legacy in adulterating its traces. It thus explores both the possibilities and the limits of Irish independence. Like *Ulysses*, it is a work of liberation, but a sceptical, even perverse one. It insists on the importance of escaping repetitive historical patterns, whilst pervasively implying that it cannot escape them itself.

This is reflected in its treatment of language. Brenda Maddox suggests that 'the universal language that Joyce created is really English with foreign touches and a strong Irish accent'.[79] Certainly, the language of the *Wake* is not a universal language, like esperanto or volapuk. It is English, but invaded on all sides. In February 1932, Joyce was still referring to Britain and Ireland together as 'Bull's islands'. He told T. S. Eliot that neither would ever 'dictate to me what and how I am to write' (*JJ*, p. 653). He claimed that 'it is my revolt against the English conventions, literary and otherwise, that is the main source of my talent'.[80] 'I am at the end of English', he told August Suter (*jj*, p. 546). He repeatedly referred to the *Wake* as a struggle with England. 'What the language will look like when I'm finished I don't know', he said. 'But having declared war I shall go on "jusqu'au bout"' (*jj*, p. 581). In the *Wake* itself, he wrote of the desire to 'wipe alley English spooker, or multiphoniaksically speaking, off the face of the erse' (*FW* 178.6–7). On winning the *Ulysses* obscenity trial in the USA, he spoke of compelling 'the English speaking world' to surrender (*jj*, p. 667). In 1936, when the British edition of *Ulysses* was finally scheduled to appear, he remarked, 'Now the war between me and England is over, and I am the conqueror' (*jj*, p. 693). He was no doubt aware of the process that, later in the same year, would conclude in the Amending Act. This would remove the presence of the British Crown and Governor-General entirely from the Irish constitution. In doing so, it would seal the transition from the Irish Free State to Éire and later the Republic of Ireland.

Joyce's linguistic practice in the *Wake* is inseparable from his declaration of cultural war. He turns the tables on the conquerors. He desecrates one of their most precious shrines. He scribbles all over the *sanctus sanctorum*, sprays it with foreign matter. Yet the more Joyce proclaimed his struggle with England, the more he announced his continuing tie to it. He himself was acutely aware of the paradox, and the *Wake* is everywhere concerned with it as a question of language. Hence the fact that the attitude of radical resistance coexists with one of radical acceptance. This is evident, above all, in the figure of Anna Livia Plurabelle, the book's most important female 'character'. Anna Livia is both a woman and the river Liffey. The *Wake* ends with her. This is appropriate enough: she is the antithesis of the world of warfare with which the book started. She does not tear things apart, but combines and recombines them. She is 'Allmahziful', a 'Bringer of Plurabilities' (*FW* 104.1–2). In an image replicating official Irish political culture, Joyce tends to leave women in a rather marginal position relative to the masculine world, though to a lesser extent than he did in *Ulysses*. But then, at the end, in a gesture oriented towards the future, he brings a woman to the fore. Anna Livia forgives her husband his sin. However, there is more than a touch of ambivalence in her attitude, and she is certainly much more than a long-suffering, relenting wife. Joyce identifies her with magnanimity, large-mindedness. From Aristotle onwards, classical Western tradition had associated this quality with a certain kind of great man. By contrast, Joyce increasingly thought of it as ordinary and female. Anna is particularly striking as an alternative to Irish culture in the 1920s and '30s, a period when real Irish-women were suffering the consequences of odiously repressive, sex-based legislation.

Finally, however, it is important to note that, in her closing soliloquy, Anna imagines visiting the Earl of Howth:

We might call on the Old Lord, what do you say? There's something tells me. He is a fine sport. Like the score and a moighty went before him. And a proper old promnentory. His door always open. For a newera's day [. . .] Remember to take off your white hat, ech? When we come in the presence. And say hoothoothoo, ithmuthisthy! His is house of laws. And I'll drop my graciast kertssey too [*FW* 623.4–11].

The first Earl of Howth (itself a 'proper old promontory') was the Norman adventurer Amory Tristram. He is of some importance in the *Wake*. In the twelfth century, at the very start of the British conquest of Ireland, he was one of the first foreigners to be granted Irish land. Anna thinks of 'the Old Lord' (and even the House of Lords) indulgently, if somewhat wryly. In the end, one must settle with one's neighbour, hereditary foe though he may long have been.

Endpiece

In 1980 Beckett paid Joyce a fabulous last tribute:

> I welcome this occasion to bow once again, before I go, deep
> down, before his heroic work, heroic being.[81]

The formality is exquisite. But why 'heroic?' It would be hard
to think of a modern writer whose vision is more anti-heroic
than Beckett's. Furthermore, Joyce shared his distaste for heroes.
Yet Beckett habitually chose his words with extreme care. It is
impossible to think that he did not do so here.

Our culture has little time for the idea of heroism, and certainly
not for the idea of intellectual heroism. We prefer celebrities.
Celebrities are better suited to democracies than heroes. Anyone
can be one. They can also be inflated and punctured indifferently.
As Joyce was only too well aware, the trouble with heroes is that
they tend to stick around, weighing 'like a nightmare on the brains
of the living'.[82] If there is a heroism worth celebrating, it is perhaps
a heroism that does not impose itself on others, but rather takes
on an imposition. This heroism is exemplified in the pursuit of
an epic inspiration or purpose. The hero or heroine becomes a
vehicle for a principle that is larger than him or herself. He or she
is spoken through, rather than speaking.

No doubt, in some ways, Joyce was narcissistic, vain and self-
seeking. Nonetheless, the man who told Claud Sykes that 'an Irish

Statue of James Joyce, Grafton Street, Dublin, 1994.

safety pin is more important than an English epic' (*JJ*, p. 423) knew exactly what he was about, and how significant it was. In *Ulysses*, Professor McHugh remarks that 'the masters of the Mediterranean are fellahin today' (*U* 7.911). One might think of this as almost a Joycean article of faith. Joyce's task was to transform if not reverse a historical structure that had conferred immense power and significance on one of two adjacent cultures, at the massive expense of the other. He undertook this task with his eyes wide open, in full acknowledgement of its labyrinthine complexities. In the process, he produced works that matched those of the very greatest English writers, and inscribed themselves in the select pantheon of European masterpieces.

Chronology

1882   Birth of James Augustine Joyce on 2 February, the eldest sur-
viving son of John Stanislaus Joyce and Mary Jane ('May')
Joyce in Rathgar, Dublin. Parnell released from arrest.
'Phoenix Park murders' of Lord Frederick Cavendish and
T. H. Burke.

1884   Foundation of Gaelic Athletic Association. James's brother
Stanislaus is born.

1886   Gladstone's Home Rule Bill defeated.

1887   John Stanislaus moves family to Bray.

1888   James enrols at Clongowes Wood College, Co. Kildare.

1889   Captain O'Shea files for divorce from his wife Katharine on
the grounds of her adultery with Parnell.

1890   Parnell ousted as leader of Irish Home Rule Party.

1891   James is removed from Clongowes. John Stanislaus loses
post as rates collector. Parnell dies. James writes 'Et Tu,
Healy', on Ireland's betrayal of Parnell.

1892   John Stanislaus moves family to Blackrock, then central
Dublin. National Literary Society founded in Ireland.

1893   Children sent briefly to Christian Brothers' School; then
James and Stanislaus enter Belvedere College. Last Joyce

child born into a family of ten. Gaelic League founded. Yeats, *The Rose* and *The Celtic Twilight*.

1894   British Prime Minister Gladstone resigns. Irish Trades Union Congress founded. John Stanislaus disposes of last Cork properties. Family moves to Drumcondra, then North Richmond Street, north Dublin.

1895   Conservative government elected in Britain, Lord Salisbury as Prime Minister.

1896   Connolly founds Irish Socialist Republican Party.

1898   Irish Local Government Act setting up elective county and district councils. Joyce's first reviews. Leaves Belvedere and enters Royal University (now University College, Dublin).

1899   Yeats, *The Wind Among the Reeds*. First production of Irish Literary Theatre. Joyce attends première of Yeats's *The Countess Cathleen*. Refuses to sign letter of protest against it.

1900   D. P. Moran founds *The Leader*. Joyce delivers paper 'Drama and Life' to University Literary and Historical Society. Writes Ibsen review, published in *Fortnightly Review*. Writes prose and verse plays, poems, epiphanies.

1901   Writes 'The Day of the Rabblement', attacking the Irish Literary Theatre. Accession of Edward VII.

1902   Leaves university and registers for Royal University Medical School. Writes Mangan essay. Reviews for Dublin *Daily Express*. 1 December leaves Dublin for Paris.

1903   Returns to Dublin for mother's illness. 3 August mother dies. Continues to write reviews. Formation of independent Orange Order. Wyndham Land Act. Longworth sacks Joyce as reviewer for the *Express*.

1904 Writes essay 'A Portrait of the Artist' and publishes three stories later included in *Dubliners*. Begins work on *Stephen Hero*. Writes and publishes poems later collected in *Chamber Music*. Leaves family home. Teaches in Clifton School, Dalkey. 10 June first meets Nora Barnacle. 16 June first walks out with her. Spends week with Oliver St John Gogarty in Martello Tower, Sandycove. On 8 October leaves Dublin with Nora, first for Zurich, then post at Berlitz School in Pola.

1905 Formation of Ulster Unionist Council. Joyce and Nora move to Trieste. Son Giorgio born. Stanislaus joins them. *Chamber Music* submitted to publishers. *Dubliners* submitted to Grant Richards.

1906 Finds post with bank in Rome. Family move there. Arthur Griffith launches *Sinn Féin*. Richards withdraws offer to publish *Dubliners*. Joyce begins 'The Dead'. First idea for story 'Ulysses'.

1907 Family returns to Trieste. Joyce writes three articles on Ireland for *Il Piccolo della Sera*. Lecture on 'Ireland, Island of Saints and Sages' at the Università del Popolo in Trieste. First eye troubles. Publication of *Chamber Music*. Daughter Lucia born. Begins rewriting *Stephen Hero* as *A Portrait of the Artist as a Young Man*. Completes 'The Dead'.

1909 Sends *Dubliners* to Maunsel & Co., and later signs contract with them. Takes Giorgio to Dublin and Galway. Returns to Trieste with sister Eva and Giorgio, then returns to Dublin to open the Volta cinema.

1910 Returns to Trieste with sister Eileen. Volta fails. Accession of George V. Publication of *Dubliners* delayed.

1911 Wrangles over *Dubliners* with George Roberts. Joyce writes open letter of complaint, published in *Sinn Féin*.

1912   Third Home Rule Bill introduced in House of Commons.
       Unionist resistance to it grows in Ulster and in Britain. Joyce
       lectures at the Università del Popolo. Writes 'L'Ombra di
       Parnell' ['The Shade of Parnell'] for *Il Piccolo della Sera*. Nora
       and Lucia and then Joyce and Giorgio travel to Ireland.
       Negotiations with Roberts fail. Joyce publishes broadside
       'Gas from a Burner'.

1913   Home Rule Bill defeated. Formation of Ulster Volunteers,
       then Citizen Army and Irish Volunteers. Joyce continues to
       lecture at the Università del Popolo. Is contacted by Ezra
       Pound.

1914   Sends Pound *Dubliners* and first chapter of *A Portrait*.
       Pound begins serialization of *A Portrait* in the *Egoist*. Grant
       Richards publishes *Dubliners*. Joyce finishes *A Portrait*, writes
       Giacomo Joyce. First World War begins. John Redmond
       pledges Irish support for British war effort. Joyce begins
       Exiles and *Ulysses*.

1915   Stanislaus arrested and interned in Austrian detention
       centre. James finishes *Exiles*. Family move to Zurich.

1916   Easter Rising in Dublin. Execution of rebel leaders. *Dubliners*
       and *A Portrait* published in New York.

1917   Publication of *A Portrait* in England. Joyce has a serious eye
       attack and undergoes his first eye operation. Harriet Shaw
       Weaver begins financial support of the family. De Valera
       elected President of Sinn Féin.

1918   Serial publication of *Ulysses* begins in the *Little Review* in
       New York. Military Service Act threatens conscription in
       Ireland. *Exiles* published by Grant Richards. Formation of
       the English Players in Zurich. Joyce quarrels with Henry
       Carr. Armistice signed. Sinn Féin win large majority of Irish
       seats in elections.

1919   Anglo-Irish War begins. De Valera elected President of Dáil Éireann. *Egoist* publishes edited versions of four chapters of *Ulysses*. *Exiles* performed in Munich. Joyce family returns to Trieste. Dáil declared illegal.

1920   Joyce family moves to Paris. Joyce meets Ezra Pound, Sylvia Beach, Valery Larbaud, T. S. Eliot, Wyndham Lewis. Final *Little Review* instalment of *Ulysses* (first part of Chapter 14) published.

1921   Editors of *Little Review* convicted of obscenity. Publication ceases. Sylvia Beach offers to publish *Ulysses*. Joyce agrees. Truce between IRA and British Army. *Ulysses* completed. Anglo-Irish Treaty signed.

1922   Dáil Éireann approves Anglo-Irish Treaty. Griffith elected President. Publication of *Ulysses*. Irish Civil War begins. Nora, Giorgio and Lucia visit Ireland, then return to Paris. Family travels to England. Joyce meets Harriet Shaw Weaver. Family return to Paris. Cosgrave elected President of Dáil.

1923   Begins *Work in Progress*. Irish Civil War ends. De Valera orders suspension of republic campaign.

1924   First fragments of *Work in Progress* published in *transatlantic review*.

1925   Effective prohibition of divorce legislation in Irish Free State.

1926   De Valera founds Fianna Fáil.

1927   Instalments of *Work in Progress* first published in *transition*. *Pomes Penyeach* published.

1929   Censorship Bill becomes law in Ireland.

1930   Giorgio marries Helen Fleischman.

1931   James and Nora marry in London. John Stanislaus dies. Foundation of Saor Éire.

1932   Son Stephen born to Giorgio and Helen Joyce. Fianna Fáil win general election in Ireland. Lucia's first breakdown.

1933   Lucia hospitalized near Zurich. Amending Acts reducing power of British crown in Éire.

1934   Random House publishes US edition of *Ulysses*. Lucia again hospitalized, and is placed in Carl Jung's care.

1935   Contraceptives made illegal in Éire.

1936   Bodley Head publishes *Ulysses* in London. Amending Act removes references to British crown and Governor-General from the Éire constitution.

1937   De Valera's new constitution approved.

1938   Helen Joyce suffers mental breakdown. Joyce finishes *Finnegans Wake*. Douglas Hyde becomes Éire's first President.

1939   Yeats dies. *Finnegans Wake* published in London and New York. Second World War begins. Éire declares itself neutral. Joyces leave Paris for St Gérand-le-Puy, near Vichy.

1940   France falls to Germany. Joyces move to Zurich.

1941   Joyce dies. Is buried in Fluntern cemetery, Zurich, with no last rites.

References

1 Ellsworth Mason, 'Ellmann's Road to Xanadu', in *Omnium Gatherum: Essays for Richard Ellmann*, ed. Susan Dick, Declan Kiberd, Dougald MacMillan and Joseph Ronsley (Gerrards Cross, 1989), pp. 4–12, p. 10.

2 Quoted in R. Barry O'Brien, *The Life of Charles Stewart Parnell*, with a preface by John E. Redmond MP (London, 1910), p. 87.

3 For further discussion, see John Wyse Jackson, with Peter Costello, *John Stanislaus Joyce: The Voluminous Life and Genius of James Joyce's Father* (London, 1997), pp. 20–23.

4 For further discussion, ibid., pp. 16–17, 37.

5 See James Connolly, *Selected Writings*, ed. P. Berresford Ellis (Harmondsworth, 1973), pp. 57–117, esp. pp. 60–64.

6 W. B. Yeats, *Autobiographies* (London, 1955), p. 554.

7 Standish O'Grady, *History of Ireland: The Heroic Period*, 2 vols (London, 1878–81), vol. II, p. 40.

8 Ibid., vol. I, p. x.

9 Lady Augusta Gregory, *The Kiltartan History Book* (Dublin, 1909), p. 51.

10 F.S.L. Lyons, *Culture and Anarchy in Ireland, 1890–1939* (Oxford, 1979), p. 57.

11 W. B. Yeats, *The Celtic Twilight: Men and Women, Dhouls and Fairies* (London, 1893), pp. 48–9.

12 Joyce followed him, giving his essay of 1912 for *Il Piccolo della Sera* the title 'L'ombra di Parnell'. See *CW*, trans. Conor Deane (Oxford, 2000), pp. 191, 336.

13 The well-known phrase was used by Gerald Balfour in 1895. See Andrew Gailey, *Ireland and the Death of Kindness: The Experience of*

Constructive Unionism, 1890–1905 (Cork, 1987), pp. 25–6.

14 'September 1913', *Yeats's Poems*, ed. A. Norman Jeffares, with an appendix by Warwick Gould (London, 1989), p. 210.

15 See Neil R. Davison, *James Joyce, 'Ulysses' and the Construction of Jewish Identity* (Cambridge, 1996), pp. 68–70.

16 See Jason Tomes, *Balfour and Foreign Policy: The International Thought of a Conservative Statesman* (Cambridge, 1997), p. 201.

17 W. B. Yeats, *Collected Letters*, vol. III (1901–4), ed. John Kelly and Ronald Schuchard (Oxford, 1994), p. 183.

18 Peter Costello, *James Joyce: The Years of Growth, 1882–1915* (London, 1992), p. 214.

19 The quotation is from the second chapter of *Ulysses*, where Deasy refers to Stephen Dedalus as a Fenian. See *Ulysses* 2.272.

20 See *CW*, p. 65.

21 See Barry, 'Introduction', in ibid., pp. ix–xxxii, p. xv.

22 Conor Cruise O'Brien, *States of Ireland* (St Albans, 1974), p. 35.

23 Brenda Maddox, *Nora: A Biography of Nora Joyce* (London, 1988), p. 314.

24 Ibid., p. 52.

25 Ibid.

26 See Costello, *James Joyce*, pp. 214–15.

27 Maddox, *Nora*, p. 109.

28 In the literature of the period, they are everywhere dubbed 'Scoti'.

29 Louis Gougaud, *Les chrétienités celtiques* (1911), quoted in J. M. Flood, *Ireland: Its Saints and Scholars* (Dublin, 1917), p. 57.

30 Stanislaus Joyce, 'Triestine Book of Days', quoted in John McCourt, *The Years of Bloom: James Joyce in Trieste, 1904–1920* (Dublin, 2001), p. 125.

31 Patrick Ward, *Exile, Emigration and Irish Writing* (Dublin, 2002), p. 28.

32 Quoted in Patrick Pearse, *The Murder Machine* (Dublin, 1916), p. 11.

33 Tomás Cardinal Ó Fiaich, 'The Beginnings of Christianity', in *The Course of Irish History*, ed. T. W. Moody and F. X. Martin (Cork, 1984), pp. 61–75, p. 74.

34 Matthew Arnold, *On the Study of Celtic Literature* (London, 1867), p. 107.

35 See Robert H. Deming, *James Joyce: The Critical Heritage*, 2 vols (London, 1970), vol. I, p. 211.

36 Sir Charles A. Cameron, *Report upon the State of Health in the City of Dublin for the Year 1903* (Dublin, 1904), p. 100.

37 R. F. Foster, *Modern Ireland, 1600–1972* (London, 1989), p. 50.

38 *A Portrait of the Artist as a Young Man*, ed. with intro. and notes by Seamus Deane (London, 1992), p. 315.

39 For Brecht's view, see Robert Weninger, 'James Joyce in German-Speaking Countries: The Early Reception, 1919–45', in *The Reception of James Joyce in Europe*, ed. Geert Lernout and Wim Van Mierlo, 2 vols (London and New York, 2004), vol. I, pp. 14–50, p. 47.

40 See *JJ*, p. 396.

41 Renzo S. Crivelli, *James Joyce: Triestine Itineraries* (Trieste, 1996), p. 34.

42 As McCourt has amply shown, in *The Years of Bloom*, pp. 41–8.

43 Ibid., pp. 103–4.

44 Ibid., p. 179.

45 Ibid., p. 218.

46 See Barry, *CW*, p. x.

47 Ibid., pp. xix–xx.

48 Ibid.

49 Quoted in ibid.

50 Quoted in 'Introduction', *Dubliners*, ed. with an introduction and notes by Jeri Johnson (Oxford, 2000), pp. xlii–iii.

51 For a full and detailed account of these sometimes modern-sounding critiques and their relation to *A Portrait*, see my essay '"That Stubborn Irish Thing": *A Portrait of the Artist* in History (i), Chapter One', in *Joyce, Ireland and Britain*, ed. Andrew Gibson and Len Platt (in preparation).

52 See *JJ*, p. 273.

53 The phrase quoted is from T. C. Barnard, *Cromwellian Ireland: English Government and Reform in Ireland, 1649–1660* (Oxford, 2000), p. 44.

54 Maddox, *Nora*, p. 69.

55 See Mark Tierney, Paul Bowen and David Fitzpatrick, 'Recruiting Posters', in *Ireland and the First World War*, ed. David Fitzpatrick (Dublin, 1988), pp. 47–58, esp. p. 48.

56 *Irish Opinion: Voice of Labour*, 26 January 1918. Quoted in Fitzpatrick, *Ireland and the First World War*, p. 81.

57 See Fitzpatrick, *Ireland and the First World War*, p. 81.

58 See *L* 2, p. 410. Bernard McGinley points out to me that the margin-

alization of the Irish delegation in the negotiations in Paris in 1919 was notably at odds with the proclaimed values of Woodrow Wilson and other victors.

59 See *SL*, p. 215.

60 Maddox, *Nora*, p. 213.

61 Letter to Olivia Shakespear. See Deming, *Critical Heritage*, vol. I, p. 284.

62 For a fuller explanation of this, see my *Joyce's Revenge* (Oxford, 2002), pp. 103–7.

63 See 'Poetry and Song, 1800–1890', in Seamus Deane, with Andrew Carpenter and Jonathan Williams, *The Field Day Anthology of Irish Writing*, 2 vols (Kerry, 1991), pp. 1–9, p. 5.

64 See Deming, *Critical Heritage*, vol. I, pp. 191, 211, 275.

65 Eric Bulson, 'Joyce Reception in Trieste: The Shade of Joyce', in Leernout and Van Mierlo, *Reception*, vol. II, pp. 311–19, p. 314.

66 Bernard McGinley, *Joyce's Lives: Uses and Abuses of the Biografiend* (London, 1996), p. 3.

67 Maddox, *Nora*, p. 259.

68 'Nineteen Hundred and Nineteen', *Yeats's Poems*, p. 315.

69 Yeats, *Uncollected Prose*, vol. II, ed. John P. Frayne and Colton Johnson (New York, 1976), p. 452.

70 Yeats, *Pages from a Diary Written in Nineteen Hundred and Thirty* (Dublin, 1944), p. 56.

71 Samuel Beckett, 'Censorship in the Saorstat', in *Disjecta: Miscellaneous Writings and a Dramatic Fragment*, ed. with a foreword by Ruby Cohn (London, 1983), pp. 84–8, p. 88.

72 Quoted in McGinley, *Joyce's Lives*, p. 13.

73 See *JJ*, pp. 640–41.

74 Joseph C. Walker, *Historical Memoirs of the Irish Bards; An Historical Essay on the Dress of the Ancient and Modern Irish; and a Memoir on the Armour and Weapons of the Irish*, 2 vols (Dublin, 1818), pp. 1, 181.

75 See, Willard Potts, ed., *Portraits of the Artist in Exile: Recollections of James Joyce by Europeans* (Dublin, 1978), p. 186.

76 In George W. Sigerson, *Bards of the Gael and Gall: Examples of the Poetic Literature of Erin* (London, 1897), p. 316.

77 The battle of Quatre Bras, referred to in the passage, might seem to be an exception. But Wellington did not win it. Indeed, somewhat ignominiously, he was forced to seek shelter to avoid capture.

78 *Yeats's Poems*, p. 411.

79 Maddox, *Nora*, p. 435.

80 Arthur Power, *The Joyce We Knew*, ed. Ulick Connor (Cork, 1967), p. 107.

81 Suheil Badi Bushrui and Bernard Benstock, eds, *James Joyce, An International Perspective: Centenary Essays of the Late Sir Desmond Cochrane*, with a message from Samuel Beckett and a foreword by Richard Ellmann (Gerrards Cross, 1982), p. vii.

82 The phrase is Marx's. See Karl Marx, *The Eighteenth Brumaire of Louis Bonaparte* (London, 1984), p. 10.

Select Bibliography

Works

Occasional, Critical and Political Writing, ed. Kevin Barry, with translations from the Italian by Conor Deane (Oxford, 2000)

Poems and Shorter Writings, Including Epiphanies, 'Giacomo Joyce' and 'A Portrait of the Artist', ed. Richard Ellmann, A. Walton Litz and John Whittier-Ferguson (London, 1991)

Dubliners, the corrected text with an explanatory note by Robert Scholes (London, 1967)

Stephen Hero, ed. Theodore Spencer, revised edn with an additional foreword by John J. Slocum and Herbert Cahoon (London, 1956)

A Portrait of the Artist as a Young Man, the definitive text corrected from the Dublin holograph by Chester G. Anderson and edited by Richard Ellmann (London, 1968)

Exiles, with the author's own notes and an intro. by Padraic Colum (Harmondsworth, 1973)

Ulysses, ed. Hans Walter Gabler, with Wolfhard Steppe and Claus Melchior, afterword by Michael Groden (New York and London, 1984, 1986)

Finnegans Wake (3rd edn, London, 1964)

Letters of James Joyce, vol. I, ed. Stuart Gilbert (London, 1957); vols II and III, ed. Richard Ellmann (London, 1966)

Selected Letters, ed. Richard Ellmann (London, 1975)

Selected Biography and Criticism

Adams, R. M., *Surface and Symbol: The Consistency of James Joyce's 'Ulysses'* (New York, 1962)

Atherton, James S., *The Books at the 'Wake': A Study of Literary Allusions in James Joyce's 'Finnegans Wake'* (revd edn, Mamaroneck, NY, 1974)

Attridge, Derek, *The Cambridge Companion to Joyce* (Cambridge, 2004)

—, *Joyce Effects: On Language, Theory and History* (Cambridge, 2000)

— and Daniel Ferrer, eds, *Post-Structuralist Joyce: Essays from the French* (Cambridge, 1984)

— and Marjorie Howes, eds, *Semicolonial Joyce* (Cambridge, 2000)

Bishop, John, *Joyce's Book of the Dark: 'Finnegans Wake'* (Madison, WI, 1986)

Boldrini, Lucia, *Joyce, Dante and the Poetics of Literary Relations* (Cambridge, 2001)

Brooker, Joseph, *Joyce's Critics: Transitions in Reading and Culture* (Madison, WI, 2004)

Brown, Richard, *James Joyce: A Post-Culturalist Perspective* (London, 1992)

—, *James Joyce and Sexuality* (Cambridge, 1985)

Brown, Terence, 'Introduction', *Dubliners*, ed. with an intro. and notes by Terence Brown (London, 1992), pp. vii–xlix

Budgen, Frank, *James Joyce and the Making of 'Ulysses'*, with an intro. by Clive Hart (Oxford, 1972)

Castle, Gregory, *Modernism and the Celtic Revival* (Cambridge, 2001)

—, 'Ousted Possibilities: Critical Histories in James Joyce's *Ulysses*', *Twentieth-Century Literature*, XXXIX/3 (Fall 1993), pp. 306–28

—, '"I Am Almosting It": History, Nature and the Will to Power in "Proteus"', *James Joyce Quarterly*, XXIX/2 (Winter 1992), pp. 281–96

Cheng, Vincent J., *Joyce, Race and Empire* (Cambridge, 1995)

—, and Timothy Martin, eds, *Joyce in Context* (Cambridge, 1992)

Colum, Padraic and Mary, *Our Friend James Joyce* (London, 1959)

Costello, Peter, 'James Joyce, *Ulysses* and the National Maternity Hospital', in Tony Farmar, *Holles Street 1894–1994: The National Maternity Hospital – A Centenary History* (Dublin, 1994), pp. 208–16

—, *James Joyce: the Years of Growth, 1882–1915* (London, 1992)

Crivelli, Renzo S., *James Joyce: Triestine Itineraries* (Trieste, 1996)

Davison, Neil R., *James Joyce, 'Ulysses' and the Construction of Jewish Identity* (Cambridge, 1996)

Deane, Seamus, 'Introduction', *A Portrait of the Artist as a Young Man*, ed. with intro. and notes by Seamus Deane (London, 1992), pp. vii–xliii

—, '"Masked with Matthew Arnold's Face": Joyce and Liberalism', in *James*

Joyce: The Centennial Symposium, ed. Morris Beja, Phillip F. Herring, Maurice Harmon and David Norris (Urbana, IL, 1986), pp. 9–21

—, 'Joyce and Stephen: the Provincial Intellectual', in *Celtic Revivals* (London, 1985), pp. 75–91

—, 'Joyce and Nationalism', in *Celtic Revivals*, pp. 92–107

Deane, Vincent, Daniel Ferrer and Gert Leernout, eds, *The Finnegans Wake Notebooks at Buffalo*, with an introduction by Vincent Deane and a bibliographic description by Luca Crispi (Turnhout, 2001–).

Deming, Robert H., *James Joyce: The Critical Heritage*, 2 vols (London, 1970)

Duffy, Enda, *The Subaltern 'Ulysses'* (London and Minneapolis, 1994)

Eide, Marian, *Ethical Joyce* (Cambridge, 2002)

Ellmann, Richard, *James Joyce* (revd edn, Oxford, 1982)

—, *The Consciousness of Joyce* (London, 1977)

—, *'Ulysses' on the Liffey* (London, 1972)

Empson, William, 'Joyce's Intentions', *Using Biography* (London, 1984), pp. 203–16

Fairhall, James, *James Joyce and the Question of History* (Cambridge, 1993)

Gibson, Andrew, *Joyce's Revenge: History, Politics and Aesthetics in 'Ulysses'* (Oxford, 2002)

— and Len Platt, eds, *Joyce, Ireland and Britain* (in preparation)

Gifford, Don, *Joyce Annotated: Notes for 'Dubliners' and 'A Portrait of the Artist as a Young Man'* (Berkeley and Los Angeles, CA, 1982)

— with Robert J. Seidman, *'Ulysses' Annotated: Notes for James Joyce's 'Ulysses'* (revised edn, Berkeley, CA, 1988)

Gilbert, Stuart, *James Joyce's 'Ulysses': A Study* (London, 1930)

Gillespie, Michael, *James Joyce's Trieste Library: A Catalogue of Materials at the Harry Ransom Humanities Research Center, University of Texas at Austin*, ed. with the assistance of Erik Bradford Stocker (Austin, TX, 1986)

—, *Inverted Volumes Improperly Arranged: James Joyce and his Trieste Library* (Ann Arbor, MI, 1983)

Groden, Michael, *'Ulysses' in Progress* (Princeton, NJ, 1977)

Hart, Clive and David Hayman, eds, *James Joyce's 'Ulysses'* (Berkeley, CA, 1974)

Hayman, David, *The 'Wake' in Transit* (Ithaca, NY, 1990)

Herr, Cheryl, *Joyce's Anatomy of Culture* (Urbana, IL, 1986)

Herring, Phillip F., *Joyce's Uncertainty Principle* (Princeton, NJ, 1987)

—, ed., *Joyce's Notes and Early Drafts for 'Ulysses': Selections from the Buffalo Collection* (Charlottesville, VA, 1977)

—, ed., *Joyce's 'Ulysses' Notesheets in the British Museum* (Charlottesville, VA, 1972)

Hofheinz, Thomas C., *Joyce and the Invention of Irish History: 'Finnegans Wake' in Context* (Cambridge, 1995)

Jackson, John Wyse with Peter Costello, *John Stanislaus Joyce: The Voluminous Life and Genius of James Joyce's Father* (London, 1997)

Janusko, Robert, *The Sources and Structures of James Joyce's 'Oxen'* (Ann Arbor, MI: 1983)

Kenner, Hugh, *Ulysses* (London, 1982)

—, *Joyce's Voices* (London, 1978)

—, *Dublin's Joyce* (London, 1955)

Kiberd, Declan, *Inventing Ireland* (London, 1995)

—, 'Introduction', *Ulysses*, ed. with an intro. and notes by Declan Kiberd (London, 1992) pp. ix–lxxx

—, 'The Vulgarity of Heroics: Joyce's *Ulysses*', in *James Joyce: An International Perspective: Centenary Essays in Honour of the Late Sir Desmond Cochrane*, ed. Suheil Badi Bushrui and Bernard Benstock, with a foreword by Richard Ellmann (Gerrards Cross, 1982), pp. 156–69

Kumar, Udaya, *The Joycean Labyrinth: Repetition, Time and Tradition in 'Ulysses'* (Oxford, 1991)

Lawrence, Karen, *The Odyssey of Style in 'Ulysses'* (Princeton, NJ, 1981)

Lernout, Geert and Wim Van Mierlo, eds, *The Reception of James Joyce in Europe*, 2 vols (London and New York, 2004)

Lowe-Evans, Mary, *Crimes Against Fecundity: Joyce and Population Control* (Syracuse, NY, 1989)

Lyons, J. B., *James Joyce and Medicine* (Dublin, 1973)

Maddox, Brenda, *Nora: A Biography of Nora Joyce* (London, 1988)

McCabe, Colin, *James Joyce and the Revolution of the Word* (2nd edn, London, 2003)

McCourt, John, *The Years of Bloom: James Joyce in Trieste, 1904–1920* (Dublin, 2001)

McGinley, Bernard, *Joyce's Lives: Uses and Abuses of the Biografiend* (London, 1996)

Mahaffey, Vicky, *States of Desire: Wilde, Yeats, Joyce and the Irish Experiment*

(Oxford, 1998)

Manganiello, Dominic, *Joyce's Politics* (London, 1980)

Morrison, Steven, 'Heresy, Heretics and Heresiarchs in the Works of James Joyce', PhD thesis, University of London, 1999

Mullin, Katherine, *James Joyce, Sexuality and Social Purity* (Cambridge, 2003)

Nadel, Ira B., *Joyce and the Jews: Culture and Texts* (Iowa City, IA, 1989)

Nolan, Emer, *James Joyce and Nationalism* (London, 1995)

Norris, Margot, *Joyce's Web: The Social Unravelling of Modernism* (Austin, TX, 1992)

Osteen, Mark, *The Economy of 'Ulysses': Making Both Ends Meet* (New York, 1995)

Parrinder, Patrick, *James Joyce* (Cambridge, 1984)

Peake, Charles, *James Joyce: The Citizen and the Artist* (London, 1977)

Pearce, Richard, *Molly Blooms: A Polylogue on 'Penelope' and Cultural Studies* (Madison, WI, 1994)

Platt, Len, *Joyce and the Anglo-Irish: A Study of Joyce and the Literary Revival* (Amsterdam and Atlanta, GA, 1998)

Potts, Willard, *Joyce and the Two Irelands* (Austin, TX, 2001)

—, ed., *Portraits of the Artist in Exile: Recollections of James Joyce by Europeans* (Dublin, 1978)

Power, Arthur, *The Joyce We Knew*, ed. by Ulick Connor (Cork, 1967)

Rabaté, Jean-Michel, *James Joyce and the Politics of Egoism* (Cambridge, 2001)

Reizbaum, Marilyn, *James Joyce's Judaic Other* (Stanford, CA, 1999)

Reynolds, Mary T., *Joyce and Dante: The Shaping Imagination* (Princeton, NJ, 1981)

Riquelme, Jean Paul, *Teller and Tale in Joyce's Fiction: Oscillating Perspectives* (Baltimore, MD, 1983)

Rose, Danis and John O'Hanlon, *Understanding 'Finnegans Wake': A Guide to the Narrative of James Joyce's Masterpiece* (New York, 1982)

Scott, Bonnie Kime, *Joyce and Feminism* (Brighton, 1984)

Senn, Fritz, *Inductive Scrutinies: Focus on Joyce*, ed. by Christine O'Neill (Dublin, 1997)

—, 'Joycean Provections', in *Joycean Occasions: Essays from the Milwaukee James Joyce Conference*, ed. Janet E. Dunleavy, Melvyn J. Friedman and Michael Patrick Gillespie (Newark, DE, 1991), pp. 171–94

—, *Joyce's Dislocations: Essays on Reading as Translation*, ed. by John Paul
    Riquelme (Baltimore, MD, and London, 1984)
Shloss, Carol, *Lucia Joyce: To Dance in the Wake* (New York, 2003)
Spoo, Robert, *James Joyce and the Language of History: Dedalus's Nightmare*
    (Oxford, 1994)
Torchiana, Donald T., *Backgrounds to Joyce's 'Dubliners'* (Boston, MA, 1986)
Tymoczko, Maria, *The Irish 'Ulysses'* (Berkeley and Los Angeles, CA, 1994)
Valente, Joseph, *James Joyce and the Problem of Justice: Negotiating Sexual
    and Colonial Difference* (Cambridge, 1995)
Van Boheemen, Christine, *Joyce, Derrida, Lacan and the Trauma of History:
    Reading, Narrative and Postcolonialism* (Cambridge, 1999)
Wales, Katie, *The Language of James Joyce* (London, 1987)
Watson, G. J., 'The Politics of *Ulysses*', in *Joyce's 'Ulysses': The Larger
    Perspective*, ed. Robert D. Newman and Weldon Thornton (Newark,
    DE, 1987), pp. 39–59

Acknowledgements

I am extremely grateful to three readers, Derek Attridge, Vicki Mahaffey and Bernard McGinley. They gave this book a great deal of their time and attention, corrected many errors, pointed out many inaccuracies and provided me with much-needed additions to and amplifications, qualifications and complications of arguments. Ian Littlewood advised me on my writing as few if any can do. Brenda Maddox provided me with some excellent advice on writing biographies over a very pleasant lunch, and Jane Lewty shared some of her expert knowledge of (Joyce and) radio with me. Deirdre Toomey was as unfailingly generous and resourceful as ever, this time, above all, with picture research. My thanks to the four of them, too. Among the staff at Reaktion, I am particularly grateful to Michael Leaman, to Vivian Constantinopoulos for all her work and great good temper, and to Harry Gilonis, the most learned picture editor an author could wish to have.

Photo Acknowledgements

The author and publishers wish to express their thanks to the following sources of illustrative material and/or permission to reproduce it.

British Museum, London (Department of Prints and Drawings): p. 34; Déri Museum, Debrecen: 43; photo courtesy of the Irish Jewish Museum, Dublin: p. 125; illustration © Josef Lada – heirs, reproduced courtesy of DILIA, Prague: p. 78; photos Library of Congress, Washington, DC (Prints and Photographs Division): pp. 53 (LC-USZ62-115280), 108 (LC-DIG-ppmsc-07948), 109 (LC-USZC4-10978), 162 (LC-DIG-ppmsc-009878); photo courtesy of the National Library of Ireland, Dublin: p. 158 (Ref. No.: LROY6196); photos Rex Features: pp. 6 (Rex Features/Everett Collection, 458358A), 12 (Rex Features/Sipa Press, 458092D), 134 (Rex Features/Csu Archiv/ Everett, 415577AT), 171 (Rex Features/George Sweeney, 233743B); photo Roger-Viollet, courtesy of Rex Features: p. 44 (© Harlingue/Roger-Viollet, RV-600843); photo courtesy of the Royal Society of Antiquaries in Ireland: p. 69.